TEMPEST.

ENJOY SHAKESPEARE

Hamlet
Julius Caesar
King Lear
Macbeth
Much Ado About Nothing
Romeo and Juliet
The Tempest
Twelfth Night

Check for new titles at www.FullMeasurePress.com

ENJOY SHAKESPEARE

The Tempest

By

William Shakespeare

A Verse Translation

By

Kent Richmond

Full Measure Press • Lakewood, California

Published by
Full Measure Press
P.O. Box 6294
Lakewood, Calif. 90714-6294 USA

www.FullMeasurePress.com

ISBN-13: 978-0-9836379-6-7

Printed in the United States of America

Contents

Illustrations

Frontispiece and illustrations on pages 14 and 49 from *Galerie des Personage de Shakspeare* (1844), compiled by Amédée Pichot (1795-1877). Paris: Baudry, Librairie Européenne. • Page 16, "Miranda—The Tempest" by John William Waterhouse (1849-1917) and page 81, "Scene with Miranda and Ferdinand" by Angelica Kauffman (1741-1807) *Wikipedia Commons.* • Pages 19, 77, 111, and 113 by Sir John Gilbert (1817-1897 from *The Gilbert Shakespeare* (1857), edited by Howard Staunton. London and New York: George Routledge & Sons. • Page 24, detail from "Tempest, Act 1, Scene 1" by George Romney (1734-1802) and engraved by B[enjamin?]. Smith from the Library of Congress (Reproduction number: LC-DIG-pga-03317). • Page 97, "Ferdinand and Miranda" by John Dawson Watson (1832-1892); engraved by Charles Mottram (1817-1886) from *The Royal Shakespeare* (1894). London, Paris, and Melbourne: Cassell and Company Limited. • Page 135, "Miranda" by John Hayter (1800-1895) from *Shakespeare in Pictorial Art* (1916) by Malcolm C. Salaman (text) and Charles Holme (ed.). London: "The Studio" Ltd. • Cover design by Kent Richmond. Stock photo of storm from Shutterstock.

About this Translation

This translation makes the language of William Shakespeare's *The Tempest* more contemporary without modernizing the play in any other way. No lines are omitted or simplified, and no characters or scenes are deleted.

My aim is for readers to experience Shakespeare's plays with the level of challenge and comprehension offered to audiences 400 years ago. Despite the richness of the plays, theatergoers in that era did not need scene summaries to follow the plot, footnotes to interpret vocabulary, or elaborate gestures to help them recognize a joke or guess at a character's intentions or emotional state. After all, Shakespeare's characters tell us what they are thinking. The plays lasted only a couple of hours, which means the actors spoke at a fairly rapid, though comfortable, pace.

To qualify this translation as authentic Shakespeare, I preserve the metrical rhythm of the original as much as possible. When the original employs iambic pentameter, this translation does too. When characters speak in prose, the translation shifts to prose. Rhymes, the occasional alliteration, and metrical irregularities are preserved. Jokes, inspired or lame, and poetic devices get modern equivalents. Sentence length and syntactic complexity are the same.

To help comprehension, I occasionally add brief pieces of exposition, careful to operate within the metrical constraints imposed by the original. Shakespeare sometimes makes references to Greek mythology, literature, and folk legends, many of which are obscure today. So "the strain of strutting Chanticleer" becomes "that rooster, strutting Chanticleer" or "said widower Aeneas too" becomes "called Dido's lover the widower Aeneas." This practice reduces the need for footnotes, which are unavailable to the theater audience and a distraction to readers. The occasional endnote offers an alternate translation of a disputed passage or explains a decision to deviate from the original. Endnotes can be ignored without loss of comprehension.

I suggest reading the translation without referring to the original so that you can imagine the play as theatre in real time with the rhythm and pacing undisturbed. Don't be surprised if the "colors" seem a bit brighter than you remember them. After four centuries, more than a little "linguistic grime" builds up as our language changes. Keep in mind how surprised we are when Renaissance paintings are restored to their original state and those muted, sepia hues turn into celebrations of color. My translation wants you to see the same colors that the ground-lings and the royalty saw when they crowded into theaters 400 years ago.

Kent Richmond

Notes on the Meter

Shakespeare's plays mix blank verse (unrhymed iambic pentameter), prose, and songs. They also include couplets or other rhyme schemes to close scenes and heighten dramatic exchanges. This translation preserves these forms, assuming Shakespeare had a dramatic justification for these swings between blank verse, prose, and rhyme.

In translating songs, I mimic the rhythm and find suitable rhymes, but Shakespeare's blank verse is more problematic and requires decisions as to what constitutes a metrical line. His plays, especially the later ones, are full of short and long lines, lines with extra syllables, and other deviations from the expected ten-syllable line. If a line deviates, was Shakespeare sloppy? Is the text corrupt? Has the pronunciation changed? Or was he aiming for some dramatic effect?

Shakespeare did not leave us polished editions of his plays. But several hundred years of tinkering by scholars has provided the polishing and copy editing that Shakespeare failed to do. I have taken advantage of that scholarship and assume that any remaining anomalies are part of Shakespeare's design and must be respected. If the deviant meter is due to pronunciation change, then I find a metrical equivalent in contemporary English. If not, then the translation deviates in the same way as the original. Expect some irregularities in *The Tempest*, especially when Prospero is speaking.

Of course no translation can perfectly capture both the sense and sound of poetry. When conflicts arise, I favor sense over strict adherence to the rhythm. Yet I do not allow a line to have a rhythm not found in Shakespeare's verse at the time he wrote the play.

For more information on Shakespeare's verse, see the article "How Iambic Pentameter Works" on page 136. For a more detailed article with exercises see www.fullmeasurepress.com.

About the Play

On June 2, 1609, the *Sea Venture* set sail from England as part of a seven-ship convoy sent to resupply the struggling British colony in Jamestown, Virginia. On July 24, a violent storm hit, separating the *Sea Venture* from the other ships and damaging the ship's hull. On August 7, the captain deliberately ran the struggling ship aground between two reefs off the shore of the uninhabited Bermuda, also called the Devil's Islands. The crew survived and over the next nine months built two new ships, restocked them, and sailed for Jamestown, arriving on May 23, 1610.

A crew lost at sea arrives at its destination 10 months later in two new ships stocked with food from a mysterious island. Combine elements of this inspirational real-life traveler's tale with Shakespeare's imagination and the result is *The Tempest*, a story about a magical island and its stranded inhabitants.[1]

The Tempest is the last known play where Shakespeare is the sole author. It was likely written sometime after news of the *Sea Venture* reached London in late 1610 and was first performed in November 1611, with one of its early performances as part of festivities preceding the wedding of the daughter of King James in 1613. The play first appeared in print as the opening play in the First Folio edition of 1623 where it was listed as a comedy.

This comedy, though the action leads towards a marriage, is not the kind of romantic comedy Shakespeare gave us in *Twelfth Night* or *Much Ado about Nothing*. In those plays, the eventual lovers are thwarted by complicated circumstances or clashes in temperament. The audience is frustrated by the many impediments and feels joy when the lovers overcome them. In *The Tempest*, the action takes place in just three hours. Shortly after a ship sailing from Tunis to Naples crashes on an island, one of the survivors, Ferdinand, meets Miranda, a teenage girl stranded there. The two immediately fall in love. Miranda's father, Prospero, who unbeknownst to them arranged their meeting, obviously approves and by Act Three is satisfied that Ferdinand is right for her. No overbearing father is forcing Miranda to marry someone she does not like. No misunderstandings threaten the courtship. No villains stand in the way.

A courtship this easy is not much to build a romantic comedy around, so Shakespeare structures the story more like what we today would call a caper film. In caper films, thieves or competing groups of thieves conspire to steal something heavily guarded, or perhaps a group of commandos undertakes a difficult mission behind enemy lines. The complicated plan delights us intellectually as do the plot twists. Often events that appear to threaten the plan or seem incidental turn out to be an integral part of it. Suspense is maintained by close calls, where characters are almost caught or killed.

In *The Tempest*, Prospero, the former duke of Milan and a student of magical arts, is the mastermind behind an elaborate caper. Left for dead at sea twelve years before with his daughter, Prospero manages to land on an island and survives with the help of two supernatural creatures, Ariel and Caliban. Ariel is a fairy spirit with impressive magical powers who is working off a debt owed to Prospero. Caliban is a half-monster, enslaved by Prospero, who knows the island's resources and does the chores. Prospero has continued studying magic and now is ready to use his powers with the help of Ariel to find a husband for his daughter and regain the dukedom stolen by his brother Antonio. Like a fun caper film, the play has its close calls and twists. The generous serving of visual effects and the spectacular onstage shipwreck are reliable crowd-pleasers.

The caper elements make the play fun but at the risk of making it also seem silly. Here is where *The Tempest's* rich poetic expression and complex themes come into play and assure its greatness. At one level, the play is a study of the interactions, behavior, and responsibilities of those who lead and those who serve. In the opening scene, as the ship approaches danger, the boatswain resents interference from nobles who seem unwilling to accept his authority aboard ship. On shore, a group of six nobles, separated from their servants and the crew, struggle to act in a way that improves their situation. King Alonso can only think of finding his missing son. The unappealing schemers, Antonio and Sebastian, resort to not-very-funny sarcasm that seems counterproductive. The scholarly Adrian makes detailed observations that may be useful, but soon the group becomes distracted by a debate over the ancient Dido's role in the history of Carthage. The optimistic Gonzalo, impressed by the island, imagines a rather unlikely utopia.

While the nobles are hamstrung by squabbling, plotting, and magical mischief, their comical servants, Stephano and Trinculo, are free to fend for themselves. They immediately see opportunities. Stephano makes a bottle out of tree bark, and upon encountering Caliban, both Trinculo and Stephano independently recognize Caliban's potential as a freak they can sell for a profit. As enterprising as Stephano seems, he is incapable of focused leadership, and we sense that Caliban is setting himself up for disappointment when he pledges his loyalty to this drunken butler. Neither group seems functional.

But it is Prospero's character and leadership that tends to attract debate. We learn from his long narratives in Act One that Prospero lost his dukedom because his interest in scholarship and magic distracted him from his duties as a duke. His dereliction leaves Antonio, his rather nasty brother, an opening to murder Prospero and usurp the dukedom. Prospero escapes to an island with his books where, for reasons explained in his narratives, he enslaves Caliban and indentures Ariel. Ariel grouses a bit but performs well. Caliban hates Prospero and wants to rape Miranda to "[people] this isle with Calibans." Powerless against Prospero's magic, Caliban feels oppressed and plots to kill Prospero. In a language Prospero and Miranda taught him, he colorfully expresses his hatred for Prospero and describes both the punishments he suffers and the charms of the island in poetry as good as that of any other character in the play. With his gift for language, we cannot help but feel some sympathy for him.

If we agree that the treatment of Caliban is cruel, does this mean that Prospero has become a slaveholding tyrant who lives for personal vengeance? For several hundred years, critics have linked this uncomfortable possibility to skepticism about the morality of European colonialism and the misery that can follow when technologically superior cultures armed with books and guns conquer and exploit. In this view, Caliban becomes a stand-in for an indigenous culture that, impressed by the knowledge and tools of European culture, naïvely gives the invader enough of a foothold to conquer and exploit the place. The notion is that Shakespeare was critical of or ambivalent toward England's recent efforts to colonize the New World and worked this theme into the play.

Shakespeare may indeed have been skeptical. The Jamestown colony had so far failed to show potential for profit except for sideshow exploitation of Indians, remarked upon by Trinculo in Act Two. But other elements of the play nibble away at the claim that *The Tempest* is an indictment of colonialism (or as some now complain, a subconscious endorsement). We must remember that every character is stranded or imprisoned there, even Caliban, and only Caliban sees it as his home. Gonzalo imagines establishing a perfect society on the isle, but he no doubt believes the place is uninhabited with no indigenous culture to exploit. A drunk Caliban proposes that Stephano rule as King, but that is a pipedream played for laughs. All arrangements are temporary. The island may simply be the author's device for holding visitors captive a few hours in a world free of the trappings of civilization.

Many students of the play feel that Prospero was based on an actual person. If true, this intention would work against the grimmer assessments of Prospero's character. Some see Prospero as modeled after King James. Surely Shakespeare did not intend to suggest that James was an enslaving tyrant. Others see Prospero as a celebration of Shakespeare himself, a magician who practices in the theatre as Prospero does on the island. Support for the Prospero-is-Shakespeare view comes from the Epilogue where Prospero, as an actor, asks the audience for applause and, as a character, asks to be set free from the island with his sins forgiven. Was Shakespeare saying goodbye to the theatre?

The Tempest leaves us with many questions. Why do we hear almost nothing from Antonio at the end of the play? Isn't it reckless for Miranda to fall for the first splendid figure she meets? Is there any importance to the chess game she and Ferdinand are playing? Why were there no women on a ship that was returning from a wedding in Tunis? These and others questions that would reveal too much of the plot nag at us. But we know to expect this of Shakespeare. He holds back just enough to keep us from reaching comfortable conclusions.

Prospero's Epilogue reminds us that the play concerns more than power, loyalty, and tyranny. It is ultimately about revenge and forgiveness. In Act One, we see that Prospero is an angry man when he explains to Miranda how they came to be on the island. Shakespeare supplies him with memorable poetry in complex, frequently rattled sentences as his powerful emotions prompt him to attempt to say too much at once. He has good reason to be angry, he possesses magical powers, and he is prepared to use them to exact revenge on those who have wronged him. But is that what happens? Be prepared for a twist. And on the printed page, where we operate without the help of actors, the twist is so sudden and understated that we may not realize what just occurred.

When John Dryden and William D'Avenant wrote an adaptation of *The Tempest*, they called it *The Enchanted Isle* (1670). That may seem a misleading or ironic title for a play where there are two murder plots and descriptions of torture, painful imprisonment, and betrayal. Yet *The Tempest* in the end is about enchantment. Eighteen times Shakespeare has his characters use the word *brave* or a derivative and intends the word to mean "splendid" rather than the more modern meaning of "courageous."[2]

And it is the world's splendidness that the more likable or redeemable characters see. Miranda sees a splendid ship, Ferdinand's splendid form, and a new and splendid world. Prospero remarks on his splendid daughter and, Ariel, his splendid spirit. Caliban sees Stephano as a splendid god for whom Miranda could provide a splendid brood. Both Stephano and Trinculo proclaim Caliban a splendid monster. The term extends to the isle, the people on it, their belongings, and the supernatural spirits who provide a sumptious banquet that magically disappears and a masque, an elaborate court pageant filled with dance and music. Eight catchy songs, enough to qualify the play as a musical, add to this celebration. And in one of the play's more surprising moments, the hate-filled monster Caliban captures this splendidness in a touching poem where he reassures Stephano and Trinculo:

> Be not afraid. The isle is full of noises,
> Sounds, and sweet tunes that give delight and hurt not.
> Sometimes a thousand strumming instruments
> Will hum around my ears, and sometimes voices,
> Though I have just awoken from long sleep,
> Will make me sleep again, and in my dreams
> The clouds will open up and drop on me
> Such riches that when I awake, I cry
> And beg to dream again.

Shakespeare, so skilled at hiding his sympathies, may have tipped his hand in his final major work. *The Tempest* looks to be a sly indictment of bitterness and sarcasm and a demonstration of how we can forgive as we embrace the splendidness of the natural world and the people in it.

Facts About The Tempest

Shakespeare's 36th play (or so)
It is the last where he was sole author.

First performance most likely in 1611
Performed for the court in 1613 as part of festivities preceding the marriage of King James' daughter Elizabeth. The masque in Act 4 may have been added for this performance.

First printed in the First Folio of Shakespeare's works (1623)
It is the opening play of the volume.

Shakespeare's 2nd shortest play
9 scenes

Just under 25% prose, with 1,359 blank verse lines, 33 epic caesurae, 67 short lines, and 19 hexameters, according to *Shakespeare's Metrical Art* (1988) by George T. Wright.

8 songs

18 speaking parts
Originally, 14 male and 4 female
Beginning in the late 17th Century, the male Ariel
was typically portrayed as female.

The *Internet Movie Database* lists just 5 films called *The Tempest* where William Shakespeare gets all or partial writing credit. Films based on or drawing from the story include the William A. Wellman western *Yellow Sky* (1946) with Gregory Peck and Anne Baxter, the sci-fi film *Forbidden Planet* (1956), *Prospero's Books* (1992), *The Tempest* (1982), a modern language adaptation by writer/director Paul Mazursky, and *The Tempest* (1998), which takes place in the antebellum South.

Other Adaptations:
The Enchanted Isle (1670) by John Dryden and William D'Avenant, followed by many adaptations often accompanied by additional songs and newly-composed incidental music.

According to the *New Grove Dictionary of Opera*,
at least 46 operas exist.
Many writers, including Percy Bysshe Shelley, Robert Browing, and W. H. Auden, have used characters or scenes as a basis for poems and stories.

Continuity problems:
A son of Antonio among the shipwrecked is mentioned in Act 1 but never appears in the play.

Sources Shakespeare used:
The story is mostly a Shakespeare original.
Passages parallel parts of two works from ancient Rome, Ovid's *Metamorphoses* and Virgil's A*eneid*. The shipwreck in Act 1 has similarities to William Strachey's account of the *Sea Venture*'s shipwreck in 1609. An essay "Of the Cannibals" by Michel de Montaigne (from John Florio's 1603 translation) provided ideas for Gonazalo's utopian vision in Act 2, Scene 1.

Shakespeare's Vocabulary:
The Tempest uses approximately 3,135 different words, with 738 words outside the 32,400 words that comprise the 6,000 most frequent word families in the British National Corpus. Kent Richmond's translation uses 3,276 different words with 495 words outside those word families.

Characters in the Play

Inhabitants of the Isle
   PROSPERO, former Duke of Milan and magician
   MIRANDA, Prospero's daughter
   ARIEL, a spirit and Prospero's servant
   CALIBAN, Prospero's servant

The Shipwrecked
   ANTONIO, Prospero's brother, current Duke of Milan
   ALONSO, King of Naples
   FERDINAND, King Alonzo's son
   SEBASTIAN, King Alonzo's brother
   GONZALO, councillor to Alonso; friend of Prospero
   ADRIAN, a lord and courtier to Alonso
   FRANCISCO, a lord and courtier to Alonso
   TRINCULO, a jester and Alonso's servant
   STEPHANO, Alonso's butler
   SHIPMASTER
   BOATSWAIN
   MARINERS

Spirits and Beings in Prospero's Masque
   IRIS
   CERES
   JUNO
   NYMPHS
   REAPERS

Other **SPIRITS** serving Prospero (as islanders and hunting
   dogs)

Scene
A ship and then an island somewhere

Line Numbers

Prose lines count as a new line whenever they break. Shared verse lines count as one line. Verse lines too long to fit on one line receive a hanging indent and count as one line.

The Tempest

Act One

Act One

Scene One. On a Ship at Sea

[The tempestuous sounds of thunder
and lightning are heard]

[Enter a SHIPMASTER and a BOATSWAIN]

SHIPMASTER
Boatswain!

BOATSWAIN
Here, master. How are you faring?

SHIPMASTER
Ah, good man! Call the mariners. On the double, or we'll
run ourselves aground. Get moving, get moving.

[Exit]

[Enter MARINERS]

BOATSWAIN
Hey, put your hearts into it, men! On the double! Take in   5
the topsail. Listen for the master's whistle. [to the wind]
You can blow till you burst if we can clear this shore.

[Enter ALONSO, SEBASTIAN, ANTONIO,
FERDINAND, GONZALO, and OTHERS]

ALONSO (King of Naples)
[knocks into the boatswain] Good boatswain, careful.
Where's the master? Act like men.

21

BOATSWAIN
It's best to keep below.   10

ANTONIO (Prospero's Brother; current Duke of Milan)
Where is the master, boatswain?

[a whistle sounds]

BOATSWAIN
Can't you hear that? You'll hamper our efforts. Stay in your cabins. You're adding to the storm.

GONZALO (a councillor to Alonso; friend of Prospero)
Now, good man, be calm.

BOATSWAIN
As soon as the sea is. Leave! Does the king's name mean   15
anything to the roaring waves crashing this place? To your cabins! Silence! Don't interfere.

GONZALO
Good man, have you forgotten who's aboard?

BOATSWAIN
No one that I love more than myself. You're on the Council. If you can command these elements to be silent and work   20
this out calmly, we will stop handling these ropes. Give your authority a try. If you cannot, then be thankful you have lived this long and prepare yourself in your cabin for the next hour's disaster if it befalls us.—[to the Mariners] Put your hearts into it, men!—[to the Courtiers] Out of   25
our way, I say.

[Exit]

GONZALO
I take great comfort in this fellow. I doubt he's marked for drowning when his manner assures himself a gallows. Keep to your plan, good Fate, and let the rope that's destined for

his hanging become our anchor since ours is of little use now.   30
If this man was not born to hang, our chances are miserable.

[Exit]
[Re-enter the BOATSWAIN]

BOATSWAIN
Down with the topmast. Quick, lower, lower! Bring her close
to the wind with the mainsail.

[He hears screaming from below]

A plague on their howling! They are louder than the weather
or the crew at work.   35

[Re-enter SEBASTIAN, ANTONIO, and GONZALO]

Not again! What are you doing here? Should we give in and
drown? Do you wish to sink?

SEBASTIAN (King Alonso's Brother)
A pox on your throat, you bawling, blasphemous, unfeel-
ing dog!

BOATSWAIN
Then get to work.   40

ANTONIO
Hang, mutt, hang, you son of a whore, you insolent noise-
maker. We are less afraid of drowning than you are.

GONZALO
I guarantee you he won't drown even if the ship's no stronger than a nutshell and as leaky as a wench without her
swathing.   45

BOATSWAIN
Closer to the wind. Set both her sails. Out to sea again.
Lay off the shore.

[Enter MARINERS, soaking wet]

All is lost! It's prayers now, prayers! All is lost!

[Exit]

BOATSWAIN
What, will we soon lie cold?

GONZALO
The King and Prince are praying. Let's assist them.   50
Our chances are the same.

SEBASTIAN
All calm has left me.

ANTONIO
Completely cheated of our lives by drunkards.

This big-mouthed rascal—[to the Boatswain] you should
  hang and then
Lie drowning through ten tides.

GONZALO
                              He'll hang unless
These drops of water open wide to gulp   55
Him down and save him from it.

> *Sounds of panic from below:* "Mercy on us!"
>   "We're splitting up!"
>   "Farewell, my wife and children!"
>   "Farewell, brother!"   60
>   "We've split. We're splitting up!"

ANTONIO
Let's all sink with the King.

SEBASTIAN
Let's say farewell to him.

                    [Exit ANTONIO and SEBASTIAN]

GONZALO
Right now I'd give a hundred miles of sea for a wretched
acre of land—thick heather, brown gorse, whatever. Thy   65
will above be done, I'd still prefer a drier death.

                            [Exit]

Scene Two. On Prospero's Island

                  [Enter PROSPERO and MIRANDA]

MIRANDA (daughter of Prospero)
If through your magic, dearest father, you've
Made the wild waters roar, now let them rest.

The sky looks set to pour down stinking tar,
But then the sea, climbing the cheeks of heaven,
Dashes the fire out. O, I have suffered   5
With those that I saw suffer! A splendid vessel,
Which no doubt had some noble creature in her,
Dashed all to pieces! O, their cries knocked hard
Against my heart itself! Poor souls, they perished.
Had I the power of a god, I would   10
Have sunk the sea beneath the earth before
It could have swallowed up the good ship and
The souls that were her cargo.

PROSPERO (former Duke of Milan and magician)
                              Calm yourself.
Be shocked no more. And tell your feeling heart
There's no harm done.

MIRANDA
                    O, woe the day!

PROSPERO
                                   No harm.   15
There's nothing here I did not do for you,
For you, my dear one, you, my daughter, who
Are ignorant of who you are, of where
I'm from, and that I had a rank much higher
Than Prospero, master of this shack and just   20
As low a father.

MIRANDA
                    Wanting to know more
Has never entered in my thoughts.

PROSPERO
                              It's time
That I inform you further. Help me to
Slip out of this magicians's robe.

                    [Lays down his robe]

                    So there

You lay, my power.—[to Miranda] Wipe your eyes. Cheer up. 25
The dreadful wreck presented here, which touched
The very essence of compassion in you,
Was managed with such foresight through my art,
So carefully arranged, that not one soul—
No, nothing so much as a strand of hair—   30
Was lost to any creature you heard cry
Aboard the vessel you saw sink. Sit down.
You must learn more about this.

MIRANDA
                                    Often you've
Begun to tell me what I am but stopped,
Concluding every fruitless inquisition   35
With "Wait. Not yet."

PROSPERO
                          The hour now has come,
The perfect time to open up your ears.
Obey, and be attentive. Can you remember
Our life before we settled in this hut?
I do not think you can, for you were not   40
Quite three years old.

MIRANDA
                          Certainly, sir, I can.

PROSPERO
Remember what? A different house, a person?
Can you describe for me an image that
Your memory still holds?

MIRANDA
                              It's far away,
More like a dream than something that assures   45
Me that my memory is true. Did four,
Perhaps five, women once take care of me?

PROSPERO
They did, and more, Miranda. But how is it

That this lives in your mind? What else is there
In the dark reaches and abyss of time?   50
If you remember anything from then,
You might recall our journey.

MIRANDA
                    But I don't.

PROSPERO
Twelve years back, Miranda, twelve years back,
Your father was the Duke of Mílan* and
A powerful prince.

MIRANDA
                    Sir, are you not my father?   55

PROSPERO
Your mother was the paragon of virtue
And said you were my daughter. And your father
Was Duke of Mílan, you his only child,
A princess no less nobly born.

MIRANDA
                    O, heavens!
What foul play could it be that sent us here?   60
Or blessing, I suppose?

PROSPERO
                    Both, both, my girl.
Through foul play, as you said, we were cast out
But blessed enough to reach here.

MIRANDA
                    O, my heart bleeds
To think of all the grief I've caused for you
Of which I have no memory. Please, go on.   65

* [translator's note] Today the English word for the Italian city Milan
has the emphasis on the final syllable, but Shakespeare wants the word
stressed on the first. Throughout the play, I add a stress mark to remind
readers of the pronunciation needed for the verse to scan properly.

PROSPERO
My brother and your uncle, named Antonio—
Please try to comprehend a brother who's
This treacherous—one whom next to you I loved
Most in this world, the one I put in charge
Of managing the state, which at that time   70
With all its provinces was at the top
And Prospero its main duke, his excellence
Renowned, his scholarship in art and science
Unparalleled. My time consumed by that,
I handed off the government to my brother   75
And grew a stranger to it, swept away,
Engrossed in studying magic. Your false uncle—
Are you still listening?

MIRANDA
                    Quite closely, sir.

PROSPERO
Having grown skilled in how to grant petitions,
How to deny them, who to sponsor, who   80
To put a leash on, he promoted or
Replaced—that's right—or altered my appointments,
And holding keys to officer and office,
He set the tune that all hearts in the state would play
To one his ear preferred and now became   85
The ivy that concealed my princely trunk
And sucked the nutrients from me. You're not listening.

MIRANDA
Good sir, I am!

PROSPERO
                    Please, try to follow this.
My steering clear of worldly aims, with full devotion
To solitude and betterment of mind,   90
Though gaining more—seclusion has its price—
Than popularly thought,¹ in my false brother
This stirred an evil nature, and my trust,
Like a good parent, was rewarded with

A falsehood, in proportion just as great   95
As my trust was, that is, without a limit,
Faith unconstrained. Advancing in this way,
Both from my income and the power that
A lord can bring to bear—like someone who
Has told so many lies against the truth   100
That his own memory's now a sinner that
Will vouch for all he says—he soon believed
He was indeed the Duke, not just a proxy
Who in my absence wore the public face
Of royalty and privilege. His ambition growing—   105
You hearing this?

MIRANDA
        Your tale, sir, would cure deafness.

PROSPERO
To raise the screen between the part he played
And he for whom he played it, Mílan he
Must rule. For me, poor man, my library was
A dukedom large enough, but he thinks I'm   110
Unfit for earthly business. Thirsting for
Some clout, he's now "cooperating" with
The King of Naples, sends him annual payments,
Pays homage, has our crown defer to his,
And has our dukedom, once unbowed—poor Mílan—   115
Contort in a disgraceful curtsy.

MIRANDA
        O heavens!

PROSPERO
Look at those terms, the outcome, then tell me
If this can be a brother.

MIRANDA
        It's a sin
To think such thoughts about my grandmother.
Good wombs can bear bad sons.

PROSPERO
Here are the terms: 120
This King of Naples, being an enemy
To me longstanding, hears my brother's offer,
Which was, that in return for terms agreed to,
Of homage, tribute—I don't know how much—
He'd clear at once down to the roots from all 125
The dukedom me and mine, and hand fair Mílan
And all its honors to my brother. Soon
A treacherous band, one midnight, picked by Fate
To fill this purpose, entered Mílan's gates—
Antonio opened them—and in dead darkness, 130
These agents, just as planned, swept in and took
Us both, with you in tears.

MIRANDA
Such heartlessness!
I, who cannot remember crying then,
Cry over it again. My eyes will be
Wrung dry by this occasion.

PROSPERO
There's still more, 135
And then I'll tell you of the present business
That's now upon us, without which this story
Would have no relevance.

MIRANDA
Why didn't they
Just slay us at that time?

PROSPERO
Good question, lass.
My tale provokes it. Dear, they did not dare— 140
So dear the people's love for me had grown—
To put a mark that bloody on this business.
In short, they painted over their foul deeds
With pretty colors, rushed us on a boat,
Took us out several miles, and put together 145
A rotten carcass of a tub—no riggings,

No tackle, sails, or mast; the rats themselves
Instinctively had left it. There they launched us,
To cry out to a sea that roared right back,
To sigh to winds that sighed back love and pity   150
Yet served to do us harm.

MIRANDA
                    Alas, what trouble
I brought you then!

PROSPERO
                O no, an angel who
Protected me! Your smile infused me with
A fortitude from heaven, which when I
Adorned the sea with drops of salty tears,   155
When I groaned from the strain, it raised in me
The stomach to endure, to push against
Whatever might ensue.[2]

MIRANDA
How did we come ashore?

PROSPERO
By Providence divine.   160
We had some food and some fresh water that
A noble Neapolitan, Gonzalo,
Gave out of charity, who having been assigned
To supervise this plan, supplied us with
Rich garments, linens, gear, necessities,   165
Quite useful things. The gentleman he is,
Knowing I loved my books, he furnished me
With works from my collection that I prize
More than my dukedom.

MIRANDA
                 I would like someday
To see this man.

PROSPERO
              It's time for me to rise.   170

[He puts on his robe]

Sit there and hear the last of our sea sorrows.
Here on this island we arrived, and here
Have I, your schoolmaster, brought you more gain
Than princes will receive, who spend their hours
On frivolous things with tutors less attentive.   175

MIRANDA
Thank heavens for it! Now, please tell me, sir,
For it's still pounding in my mind, why you
Have caused this storm at sea?

PROSPERO
                          I'll say this much:
Through some strange chance, that generous goddess,
    Fortune,
Now my dear friend, has brought my enemies   180
Here to this shore; and through my premonition
I've found the zenith of my fate rides on
A star quite favorable, an influence
I should pursue and not neglect, for soon
My fortune will descend. No further questions.   185
You'll want to sleep—a drowsiness that's good,
So yield to it. I know you cannot help it.

[MIRANDA sleeps]

[to Ariel] Come to me, servant, come. I'm ready now.
Approach, my Ariel. Come.

[Enter ARIEL]

ARIEL (a spirit and Prospero's servant)
All hail, great, learnèd master! Hail! I come   190
To do for you what pleases best—to fly,
To swim, to dive into the fire, to ride
On the curled clouds. Send Ariel and his assets
To do your mighty bidding.

PROSPERO
                              Did you, spirit,
Produce the tempest just as I had ordered?   195

ARIEL
In every detail.
I boarded the King's ship; first on the bow,
Then midship, then the deck, in every cabin,
I stunned them with my flames. I'd sometimes split
And burn in many places. On the topmast,   200
The yards, and bowsprit, separately I'd flash,
Then meet and join. Jove's lightning, heralding
The dreaded thunder-claps, was not more fleeting
Or quicker for the eye. The cracking fire,
The sulphurous roar laid seige to mighty Neptune   205
And seemed to make his bold waves tremble and
His dreaded trident shake.

PROSPERO
                              My splendid spirit!
Were any firm, so steady that this chaos
Did not infect their reason?

ARIEL
                              Every soul
There felt the frenzy of a madman and   210
Committed desperate acts. All but the mariners
Plunged in the foaming brine and quit the vessel,
Surrounded by my fire. The King's son, Ferdinand,
With hair on end—straight up, like reeds, not hair—
Was first to leap and cried "Hell's empty now,   215
And all its devils here."

PROSPERO
                              Yes, that's my spirit!
And this was near the shore?

ARIEL
                              Close by, my master.

PROSPERO
But, Ariel, are they safe?

ARIEL
              Not one hair perished.
And on the clothes that buoyed them, not a blemish,
And cleaner than before; and, as you ordered,   220
They are dispersed in groups around the isle.
I had the King's son land all by himself
And left him cooling down the air with sighs
In some odd corner of the island— sitting,
Arms sadly folded.

PROSPERO
             What of the King's ship,   225
Its sailors, and the fleet? Where have you placed
The rest of them?

ARIEL
            They're safe. The King's ship's in
The harbor, hidden in the deep nook where
You summoned me at midnight once to fetch
Some dewdrops from Bermuda's storm-wracked air;   230
The mariners, all stowed below the deck,
Charmed by a spell, are sleeping off the labors
They suffered; the remainder of the fleet,
Has been dispersed and will regroup out in
The Mediterranean sea where, saddened, they   235
Are bound for home in Naples,
Believing that they saw the King's ship wrecked
And their great leader perish.

PROSPERO
               Exactly as
I ordered, Ariel, but there's more work.
What is the time of day?

ARIEL
            It is past noon.   240

PROSPERO
At least two hours. The time from now till six,
The two of us must spend it carefully.

ARIEL
Is there more work? Since you give me these tasks,
Let me remind you of your promise to me,
One you have not fulfilled.

PROSPERO
                        What's this? Resentment?   245
What is it that you want?

ARIEL
                My liberty.

PROSPERO
Before the time is up? Enough!

ARIEL
                        Consider
The value of the work I've done for you.
I've told no lies, made no mistakes, and served
Without a gripe or grumble. You promised to   250
Release me one year early.

PROSPERO
                        Don't forget
What torment I have freed you from.

ARIEL
                        I haven't.

PROSPERO
You have and think that trudging through some slime
Along the ocean floor,
Or running up a sharp wind from the north,   255
Or digging through a vein of frost-baked earth
Now asks too much of you.

ARIEL
               I do not, sir.

PROSPERO
You lying, malignant thing. Have you forgotten
The foul witch Sycorax, whose age and malice
Bent her into a hoop? Have you forgotten?   260

ARIEL
No, sir.

PROSPERO
          You have. Where was she born? Speak. Tell me.

ARIEL
Sir, in Algiers.

PROSPERO
             You do recall. Yet I
Must every month recount what you have been
Or you'll forget—that Sycorax, condemned
For countless crimes and sorceries too appalling   265
To share with human ears, was, as you know,
A witch tossed from Algiers whose life was spared
Because she'd done one thing. Is that not so?

ARIEL
Yes, sir.

PROSPERO
This hag with blue-ringed eyes, shipped off with child,   270
Was left here by the sailors. You, my slave,
Were at that time, as you've described, her servant,
And since you were a spirit too exquisite
To carry out her gross and horrid orders,
Refusing grand requests, she then confined you,   275
With help from the more potent of her agents
And in a rage too great to be appeased,
Inside a cleft within a pine in which
You painfully remained imprisoned for

A dozen years, a space of time in which   280
She died and left you there to pour out groans
Like water from a mill. The island, then,
Had she not dropped a son—a spotted pup,
Hag-born—would not have had a human shape
To grace it.

ARIEL
                    You mean Caliban, her son.   285

PROSPERO
Of course, you dullard.[3] Yes, the Caliban
I keep to serve me now. You know too well
The torment that I found you in. Your groans
Caused wolves to howl and pierced into the hearts
Of always-angry bears. It was a torment   290
That's laid upon the damned, one Sycorax
Could not undo again. It was my power,
When I arrived and heard you, that split wide
The pine and let you out.

ARIEL
                    I thank you, master.

PROSPERO
One more complaint and I will split an oak   295
And tack you to its knotted entrails till
You've howled twelve winters straight.

ARIEL
                              Forgive me, master.
I will comply with all commands and do
My spritely tasks without complaint.

PROSPERO
Do so, and after two days   300
I will discharge you.

ARIEL
                    That's my noble master!
What must I do? What must I do? Just name it.

PROSPERO
Go turn yourself into a sea nymph now,
Perceived by none but you and me, invisible
To every other eye. Use this disguise,   305

[Hands ARIEL a garment]

And come back in it. Do it immediately![4]

[Exit ARIEL]

[to Miranda] Awake, dear heart, awake. You have slept well.
Awake.

MIRANDA
          The strangeness of your story must
Have made me drowsy.

PROSPERO
                    Shake it off. Come on,
We'll visit Caliban, my slave, who's yet   310
To greet us kindly.

MIRANDA
                    He's the lowest, sir,
One I don't care to look at.

PROSPERO
                    As it stands,
We need him here. It's he who makes our fire,
Fetches our wood, and works at many tasks
That profit us. What ho! Slave! Caliban!   315
Earth creature! Speak.

CALIBAN (Prospero's servant)
          [inside his dwelling] There's wood enough inside.

PROSPERO
Come out, I say. There's other work for you.
Come out, you tortoise! Move.

[Re-enter ARIEL, as a water-nymph]

A fine illusion, clever Ariel.
Give me your ear.

[Whispers in ARIEL'S ear]

ARIEL

      My lord, it shall be done.   320

[Exit]

PROSPERO
[to Caliban] You poisonous slave, sired when the devil
    himself
Fell on your wicked dam. Come out!

[Enter CALIBAN]

CALIBAN
May dew as foul as mother ever brushed
With raven's feathers from some putrid swamp
Drop on you both! And toxic winds blow on you   325
And blister you all over!

PROSPERO
For that, be sure, tonight you shall have cramps
And stitches in your side that stop your breath,
While spiny goblins through a ceaseless night
Find work to do and punch you with more holes   330
Than in a honeycomb, each stinging more
Than any bee does.

CALIBAN
          I must eat my dinner.
This island's mine, from Sycorax my mother,
Which you took from me. When you first arrived,
You stroked me and did much for me, you'd give me   335
Water with berries in it, teach me what
To call the bigger light and lesser one

That burns both day and night. And then I loved you
And showed you all the island's resources,
The fresh springs, salt-pits, barren spots, what's fertile.   340
And now I'm cursed for it! May all the spells
Of Sycorax—toads, beetles, bats—land on you!
The only subject that you have is one
Who once was his own king. And here you pen
Me up in this hard rock where I am kept   345
Away from most the isle.

PROSPERO
               You lying slave,
Who's roused by whips, not kindness! You've been treated,
Despite your filth, humanely, and I lodged you
In my own room until you tried to violate
The honor of my child.   350

CALIBAN
Oh ho, oh ho! And wish it had been done.
But you prevented it or I'd have filled
This isle with Calibans.

MIRANDA
             Disgusting slave,
On whom no mark of goodness can be stamped,
Disposed toward all that's wrong! I pitied you,   355
Took pains to give you speech, taught you each hour
One thing and then the next. You, savage, whose
Own sounds you couldn't grasp and gabbled like
Some brutish thing, yet I sensed your intent
And furnished you with words. But your vile stock,   360
Though you could learn, has something in it that
The good cannot abide, and thus you were
Deservedly restricted to this rock,
Though you deserved much worse than prison.

CALIBAN
You taught me language, and my profit is   365
That I know how to curse. The red plague wreck you
For teaching me your language!

PROSPERO
                    Hag-seed, go!
Fetch us some fuel. Be quick, and if you're smart,
You'll get on with your chores. You shrug, you malice?
If you neglect or do what I command   370
Unwillingly, I'll torture you with cramps,
Fill all your bones with aches, and make you roar
With such a din that beasts will tremble.

CALIBAN
                                   Please, no.
[aside] I must obey. His magic has such power
That even Setebos, my mother's god,   375
Would yield and have to serve him.

PROSPERO
                         Then, slave, go!

               [Exit CALIBAN]

     [Enter FERDINAND and ARIEL, invisible to him,
                 playing and singing]

ARIEL
[sings] *Come unto these yellow sands,*
     And then take hands.
A kiss and curtsy, if you please,
     The wild waves ease.   380
Deftly dance it here and there,
And, sweet sprites, the chorus share.
     Hark, hark!

[A random chorus of "Bow-wows" is heard from offstage]

     The watch dogs bark.

          [More "Bow-wows" are heard]

     Hark, hark! I hear   385
That rooster, strutting Chanticleer,
     Cry cock-a-diddle-dow.

FERDINAND (King Alonso's son)
This music, where's it from? The air? The earth?
It's gone but must be in the service of
Some god that dwells here. Sitting on a bank,   390
And mourning still the loss of King and father,
This music wafted by me from the water,
Allaying both its fury and my suffering
With its sweet tune. I followed it, or I
Should say, it led me here. But now it's gone.   395
No, there it is again.

ARIEL'S SONG
   Five fathoms down your father lies.
    From his bones is coral made.
   Those are pearls that were his eyes.
    The parts of him that soon will fade   400
   Will undergo a sea-change
   And turn to something rich and strange.
   Each hour sea nymphs ring his knell.

[A chorus is heard: "Ding-dong"]

Hark! Now I hear them—Ding-dong bell.

FERDINAND
The song's commemorating my drowned father.   405
There's nothing human here, nor is this sound
Owned by this world. I hear it now above me.

PROSPERO
Draw back the curtains that adorn your eyes
And tell me what you see.

MIRANDA
               What's this? A spirit?
Lord, how it looks around! Believe me, sir,   410
It has a splendid form. But it's a spirit.

PROSPERO
No, girl, it eats and sleeps; it's senses are

The same as ours. This gentleman you see
Was in the wreck. He's somewhat marked with grief,
And it gnaws at his looks, but that aside,   415
A handsome man. He lost all his companions
And roams in search of them.

MIRANDA
                              I'd say he is
A thing divine, for nothing nature's shown
To me has seemed so noble.

PROSPERO
                              [aside] It works, I see,
As I suspected. [to Ariel] Spirit, fine spirit, I'll free   420
You in two days for this.

FERDINAND
                    [seeing Miranda] No doubt, the goddess
These songs are meant to serve!—Please deign to answer
So I may know if you dwell on this island
And give me some instruction as to how
To best conduct myself. My prime request,   425
The last I'll make, is if you are—O wonder!—
A maiden of this world?

MIRANDA
                           I am no wonder
But certainly a maiden, sir.

FERDINAND
                         My language?
Heavens! I'd be the highest ranking speaker
If I were where it's spoken.

PROSPERO
                              What? The highest?   430
What if the King of Naples heard you say this?

FERDINAND
And now one and the same,[5] amazed to hear

You speak of Naples' King. He hears himself
And that is why I weep—I'm now that king—
With eyes, whose tide has yet to ebb, that saw   435
The King, my father, perish.

MIRANDA
                              May God have mercy!

FERDINAND
Indeed, with all his lords, the Duke of Mílan,
His splendid son as well.[6]

PROSPERO
                    [aside] The Duke himself
And his more splendid daughter could dispute this
If now the time were fitting. At first sight   440
These two locked eyes. Exquisite Ariel,
I'll set you free for this. [to Ferdinand] A word, good sir.
I fear you've done yourself some harm. A word.

MIRANDA
Why are my father's words so rough? This is
The third man that I've ever seen, the first   445
I've ever sighed for. May compassion sway
My father to support me.

FERDINAND
                    If unmarried
With fondness pledged to no one else, I'll make you
The Queen of Naples.

PROSPERO
                    Wait, sir! One more word.
[aside] They're in each other's power, but I must add   450
A snag to this quick deal; a prize seems cheap
If won too cheaply. [to Ferdinand] One more word. Hear
    what
I have to say. You've staked a claim here to
A title you don't own and placed yourself
Upon this island as a spy, to take it   455
From me, its lord.

FERDINAND
No, as a man, I swear it.

MIRANDA
No wickedness could dwell in such a temple.
A wicked spirit could not keep the good
From dwelling in so fine a house.

PROSPERO
[to Ferdinand] Just follow.
[to Miranda] Don't speak for him. He is a traitor. [to
    Ferdinand] Come.   460
I'll manacle your neck and feet together.
Sea-water you will drink. Your food shall be
Poisonous mussels, withered roots, and husks
That cradle acorns. Follow me.

FERDINAND
I won't.
Such treatment I'll resist until I see   465
An enemy more powerful.

[He draws his sword but is frozen by a spell]

MIRANDA
Dear father,
Don't be too rash in testing him, for he
Is noble and won't cower.[7]

PROSPERO
[to Miranda] What's this? My foot
Is now my tutor? [to Ferdinand] Traitor, sheathe your sword.
A show of arms without a strike reveals   470
A conscience full of guilt. Relax your stance.
I'm able to disarm you with this wand
And make your weapon drop.

MIRANDA
I beg you, father!

PROSPERO
Go! Don't hang on my clothing.

MIRANDA
                              Sir, have pity.
I'll be his guarantor.

PROSPERO
                         Silence! One word more   475
And I will scold you, if not hate you. What?
You'll be defending an imposter! Hush!
You think that he alone is shaped this way—
You've seen just him and Caliban. You fool!
Against most other men, he's Caliban.   480
Compared to him, they're angels.

MIRANDA
                                   I'm quite humble
In my affections. I do not desire
A finer-looking man.

PROSPERO
                       [to Ferdinand] Come on. Obey.
Your muscles are in infancy again
And have no vigor in them.

FERDINAND
                            So they are.   485
My energy's bound up, as in a dream.
My father's death, the weakness that I feel,
The loss of all my friends, and this man's threats,
Which I must bear, would be light punishment
If from my prison once a day I could   490
Behold this maid. Each corner of this earth
The free are welcome to. This prison here
Has space enough for me.

PROSPERO
                          [aside] It's working. [to Ferdinand]
     Come.—

[to Ariel] You have done well, fine Ariel! [to Ferdinand]
    Follow me.
[to Ariel] Here is what else you'll do for me.

MIRANDA

                        Cheer up.   495
My father has a better nature, sir,
Than you'll sense from his speech. What you just saw
Is out of character.

PROSPERO

             [to Ariel] You'll be as free
As mountain winds. For that to be, do all
That I've commanded.

ARIEL

             Every syllable.   500

PROSPERO

[to Ferdinand] Come along. [to Miranda] Don't speak for
    him.

               [Exit]

The Tempest

Act Two

Act Two

Scene One. Another Part of the Island

[Enter ALONSO, SEBASTIAN, ANTONIO, GONZALO,
ADRIAN, FRANCISCO, and OTHERS]

GONZALO
Please, sir, cheer up. You have much cause for joy,
As do we all, for our escape leaves us
More than we lost. Occasions for such woe
Are commonplace; each day, some sailor's wife,
The captain of some merchant ship, its owner,   5
Have these same grounds for woe, but we miraculously
Survived—a few picked from unlucky millions
Can ever say this. Sir, it's wise to weigh
Our grief against such charity.

ALONSO
                                                Please, enough.

SEBASTIAN
[aside to Antonio] To him, charity means another helping   10
of cold porridge.

   [As the scene continues, Antonio and Sebastian speak
      privately but loudly enough to be overheard] [1]

ANTONIO
But our sister of mercy won't be turned away that easily.

SEBASTIAN
Look, he's winding up the watch of his wisdom. It's about
to chime.

51

GONZALO
[to Alonso] Sir—   15

SEBASTIAN
One. Count with me.

GONZALO
When every grief that visits us is welcomed, what comes
to the welcomer is—

SEBASTIAN
The bill for it.

GONZALO
It takes its toll, indeed. Your words are truer than you   20
realize.

SEBASTIAN
You found more wisdom in them than I intended.

GONZALO
[to Alonso] Therefore, my lord—

ANTONIO
Shame on him, to spend his words so lavishly!

ALONSO
[to Gonzalo] Please, stop.   25

GONZALO
Well, I will, but still—

SEBASTIAN
[aside to Antonio] He'll keep on talking.

ANTONIO
[aside to Sebastian] Which of these two would you wager,
he or Adrian, will be the first to crow?

SEBASTIAN
I'll take the old rooster.   30

ANTONIO
I'll take the young one.

SEBASTIAN
Done. The wager?

ANTONIO
The last laugh or the eggs if any.

SEBASTIAN
Agreed!

ADRIAN (a lord and courtier to Alonso)
Though this island seems to be deserted—   35

ANTONIO
Ha, ha, ha!

SEBASTIAN
You just took your payment.

ADRIAN
Uninhabitable, and almost inaccessible—

SEBASTIAN
Yet—

ADRIAN
Yet—   40

ANTONIO
I knew he'd say that.

ADRIAN
It clearly has a climate that is a fresh, pleasing example
of temperance.

ANTONIO
Temperance, she was a pleasing wench.

SEBASTIAN
Yes, and fresh, as he so learnedly expressed.   45

ADRIAN
The air breathes upon us here quite sweetly.

SEBASTIAN
As if it had lungs, full of rot.

ANTONIO
Or, as if perfumed by a swamp.

GONZALO
Here everything is advantageous to life.

ANTONIO
True, unless one actually lives here.   50

SEBASTIAN
Little or no chance of that.

GONZALO
How lush and luxurious the grass looks! How green!

ANTONIO
I'd say the land is tawny.

SEBASTIAN
But with a hint of green in it.

ANTONIO
He wasn't off by much.   55

SEBASTIAN
No, yet manages to miss the truth entirely.

GONZALO
But the oddest thing, which is indeed almost beyond
belief—

SEBASTIAN
The tales these travelers tell.

GONZALO
Is that our garments, despite being, as they were, drenched   60
in the sea, have retained their brightness and luster, as if
freshly dyed, when they should be soaked with salt water.

ANTONIO
If one of his soggy pockets could speak the truth, wouldn't
it say he's lying?

SEBASTIAN
Yes, but a pocket can only hold the truth.   65

GONZALO
It seems to me our garments are as fresh now as when we
first put them on in Africa, at the marriage of the King's
fair daughter Claribel to the King of Tunis.

SEBASTIAN
It was a sweet marriage, and we will prosper when we
return.   70

ADRIAN
Tunis has never been graced with such an ideal queen.

GONZALO
Not since the widow Dido fled there to found it.[2]

ANTONIO
Widow! A pox on that! Why add the word widow? Some
widow!

SEBASTIAN
What if he had called Dido's lover the "widower Aeneas?"   75
Lord, you take things hard!

ADRIAN
[to Gonzalo] "Widow Dido" did you say? That deserves some
study. She was from Carthage, not Tunis.

GONZALO
Tunis, sir, was once Carthage.

ADRIAN
Carthage?   80

GONZALO
I assure you, Carthage.

ANTONIO
His words outdo the miraculous harp that built the walls
of ancient Thebes.

SEBASTIAN
And he builds more than walls. Houses too.

ANTONIO
What's the next impossible task that he'll make easy?   85

SEBASTIAN
I think he will carry this island home in his pocket and
give it to his son for an apple.

ANTONIO
And sowing its seeds in the sea, he'll bring forth more
islands.

GONZALO
[to Adrian] I—   90

ANTONIO
For once you agree.

GONZALO
[to Alonso] Sir, we were saying that our garments seem as
fresh now as when we were at Tunis at the marriage of
your daughter, who is now Queen.

ANTONIO
And the finest one that ever lived there.   95

SEBASTIAN
Please don't bring up widow Dido again.

ANTONIO
O, widow Dido! That's right, widow Dido.

GONZALO
[to Alonso] Isn't my doublet, sir, as fresh as the first day I
wore it? I mean, considering.

ANTONIO
You do plenty of that.³   100

GONZALO
[to Alonso] When I wore it at your daughter's marriage.

ALONSO
You cram words in my ear when I don't have
The stomach for them. Now I wish that she
Had never married there; by coming here,
I've lost my son, and if I'm right, she too,   105
For she's so far removed from Italy
I won't see her again. My son, the heir
To Naples' throne and Mílan's, what strange fish
Have made a meal of you?

FRANCISCO (a lord and courtier to Alonso)
                              He may have lived, sir.
I saw him beat against the surging waves   110
And ride upon their backs. He flung the sea's
Hostility aside and threw his breast against
The swelling surge that met him. His bold head
He kept above the wave's assault and rowed
Himself with his strong arms and mighty strokes   115
To where the wave-worn shoreline's cliff stooped down
As if to rescue him. I have no doubt
He reached the land alive.

ALONSO

No, no, he's gone.

SEBASTIAN
Sir, you can thank yourself for this great loss.
Instead of blessing Europe with your daughter,   120
You farmed her out to Africa where she,
To say the least, is banished from your eye,
Which you made wet with sorrow.

ALONSO

Please, enough.

SEBASTIAN
We kneeled before you and implored you to
Do otherwise, and the fair soul herself   125
Weighed loathing and obedience to see
Which way the scale would tip. We've lost your son,
I fear, for good. Naples and Mílan have
More widows in them, owing to this business,
Than we have men with which to comfort them.   130
The fault's your own.

ALONSO

As is the heaviest loss.

GONZALO
My lord Sebastian,
The truth you speak could be more delicate
And at a different time. You rub the sore
When you should put a dressing on it.

SEBASTIAN

Fine.   135

ANTONIO
Just like a surgeon.

GONZALO
[to Alonso] It is foul weather for us all, good sir,
When you are cloudy.

SEBASTIAN
Foul weather?

ANTONIO
[looks at the sky] Very foul.

GONZALO
Granted the right to colonize this isle—

ANTONIO
With termites—

SEBASTIAN
Ants, or bees, I have no doubt.   140

GONZALO
—And if I were its king, what would I do?

SEBASTIAN
You'd sober up since there's no wine.

GONZALO
I'd build the commonwealth with actions that
Ignore all custom. I'd permit no kind
Of commerce and no government officials;   145
No records would be kept; wealth, poverty
And use of servants, none; contracts, inheritance,
Deeds, boundaries, farms and vineyards, none;
No use of metal, corn, or wine, or oil;
No jobs and all men free from labor, all,   150
And women too, yet innocent and pure;
No rank or class—

SEBASTIAN
Yet he would be its king.

ANTONIO
This end of his commonwealth forgot how it started.

GONZALO
And all production held for general use,
Made without sweat or toil. And treason, felony, 155
Swords, pikes, knives, guns, machinery of all types,
I would not have, but nature on its own
Would bring about profusion and abundance
To feed my innocent people.

SEBASTIAN
No marrying among his subjects? 160

ANTONIO
None, man. Just good-for-nothings, whores, and knaves.

GONZALO
With such perfection I would govern, sir,
And would surpass the Golden Age.

SEBASTIAN
God save his Majesty!

ANTONIO
                    Long live Gonzalo!

GONZALO
And were you listening, sir? 165

ALONSO
No more, please. All this talk means nothing to me.

GONZALO
And I believe your Highness, but it did provide an opportunity for these gentlemen to continue their habit of using their swift and agile lungs to laugh at nothing.

ANTONIO
It was you we laughed at. 170

GONZALO
And since this kind of merry clowning suggests I am nothing to you, you are free to continue laughing at nothing.

ANTONIO
What a blow he gave us there!

SEBASTIAN
If he hadn't used the flat edge of the blade.

GONZALO
The splendid mettle you gentlemen display. If only the   175
moon's orbit took five weeks instead of four, why you'd have
stolen her by now.

     [Enter ARIEL, invisible, playing solemn music]

SEBASTIAN
And used it as a lantern to catch sleeping birds.

ANTONIO
My good lord, you're not angry with us?

GONZALO
No, I assure you. I do not wish to jeopardize my composure   180
over little things. Will you laugh me to sleep? I'm feeling
very heavy.

ANTONIO
Go to sleep. You'll hear plenty.

     [Everyone sleeps except for ALONSO,
       SEBASTIAN, and ANTONIO]

ALONSO
What, all so soon asleep! I wish my eyes
By closing could shut down my thoughts as well.   185
They seem inclined to do so.

SEBASTIAN
              Let them, sir.
Accept the break that heaviness provides.
It seldom comes with sorrow. When it does,
It's there to comfort us.

ANTONIO
> The two of us,
My lord, will guard you while you rest and keep   190
You safe.

ALONSO
> Thank you—this heaviness astounds me.

> [ALONSO sleeps. Exit ARIEL]

SEBASTIAN
What a strange drowsiness possesses them!

ANTONIO
The climate is affecting them.

SEBASTIAN
> And yet
Our eyelids are not drooping. Why? I feel
No urge to sleep.

ANTONIO
> Same here. My mind's alert.   195
They all dropped off as if by some agreement,
As if struck by a thunderbolt. Could this,
Worthy Sebastian? O, could this? Enough!
And yet I sense I'm seeing in your face
What you might be. The situation and   200
My strong imagination say a crown
May soon drop on your head.

SEBASTIAN
> Are you awake?

ANTONIO
Did you hear what I said?

SEBASTIAN
> I did but must
Be half asleep, or you were talking in

Your sleep. What was it that you said just now?   205
A weird repose this is, to be asleep
With eyes wide open, standing, speaking, moving,
And yet so fast asleep.

ANTONIO
     Noble Sebastian,
You'd let your future sleep—no, die and wear
A blindfold when awake.

SEBASTIAN
       Your snores make sense.   210
There's more than snoring here.

ANTONIO
I'm being serious for once, and you
Should too. Just hear me out and you will see
Your fortunes triple.

SEBASTIAN
     I'm a stagnant pond.

ANTONIO
I'll show you how to flow.

SEBASTIAN
       Good luck. Sloth is   215
My birthright—it tells me to ebb.

ANTONIO
      O, if
You'd only see that mockery reveals
How much you want this, that by stripping it
You dress it finer. Yes, when fortunes ebb
And men run near the bottom, mostly it   220
Is due to their own fear or sloth.

SEBASTIAN
      Go on.
The way you've fixed your eyes and cheeks suggest

That you're delivering something vital here,
And it's a painful birth.

ANTONIO
                              It's like this, sir:
[gestures toward Gonzalo] This lord, whose weakened
    memory can hold   225
No more than we'll recall of him once he's
Been laid to rest, has just about convinced
The King—he is by trade a master of
Persuasion—that his son's alive though it's
More likely sleeping men can swim than he   230
Escaped this drowning.

SEBASTIAN
                              There is little hope
That he's not drowned.

ANTONIO
                              And from such little hope
What great hope is to come! No hope for one
Means higher hopes for someone else, so high
Ambitious men who peek that far ahead   235
Doubt what's revealed.[4]

SEBASTIAN
                              I'm lost.

ANTONIO
                              Do you agree
That Ferdinand has drowned?

SEBASTIAN
                              He's gone.

ANTONIO
                                       Then tell me,
Who's next in line in Naples?

SEBASTIAN
> Claribel.

ANTONIO
The Queen of Tunis—who's a lifetime and
A day away; who can't get mail from Naples   240
Before there's stubble on a newborn's chin
Unless the sun delivers it—the Man in
The Moon's too slow; who'll think her wedding guests
Were swallowed by the sea, except that fate
Has cast some of us here to do a show   245
Where past is prologue, and what's yet to come
Will be produced by you and me.

SEBASTIAN
What is all this? What are you saying?
It's true, my brother's daughter's Queen of Tunis
And heir to Naples throne, two regions with   250
Some space between them.

ANTONIO
> And each foot of it
Seems to cry out "And how will Claribel
Traverse this stretch between them? Stay in Tunis
And let Sebastian wake." Suppose that this
Were death that seized them. [points to the sleeping men]
> They'd be no worse off   255
Than they are now. And others could rule Naples
As well as this one here, or prattle on
As constantly and needlessly as this
Gonzalo. I myself could get a crow
To chat this deeply. O, if you embraced   260
These thoughts of mine, think what this sleep could do
For your advancement! Do you understand me?

SEBASTIAN
I guess I do.

ANTONIO
> And how are you inclined
To view your own good fortune?

SEBASTIAN
                                  I remember
That you displaced your brother Prospero.

ANTONIO
                                        True.   265
And look how well these garments sit upon me,
More fitting than before. My brother's servants
Were once my peers, but now they are my servants.

SEBASTIAN
But, what about your conscience?

ANTONIO
And where's that found, sir? If it caused sore heels,   270
I'd be in slippers. My bosom doesn't feel
Such righteousness, and twenty consciences
Between me and this king, preserved in ice,
Would melt and not impede me. There's your brother,
No better than the earth he lies upon.   275
If he were what he looks like now—yes, dead—
I could with just three inches of this trusted steel
Put him to bed for good, while you, like this, [mimics a
    sword thrust]
Could place an everlasting lid upon
These ancient scraps, Sir Prudence here, and end   280
His censure of our actions. And the rest?
They'll lap up our enticements as a cat
Does milk. They'll set their clocks to coincide
With what we plan.

SEBASTIAN
                        Your case, dear friend, will be
My precedent. The way that you got Mílan,   285
I'll use for Naples. Draw your sword. One stroke
Will free you from the tribute you must pay,
And I the King shall favor you.

ANTONIO
                              Together

We'll draw and when I raise my hand, raise yours
To fall upon Gonzalo.

SEBASTIAN
　　　　　　First, one more thing.　　　　　　290

[Antonio and Sebastian talk separately as ARIEL,
invisible to them, re-enters with music and song]

ARIEL
My master's wizardry foresees the danger
That you, his friend, are in, and sends me here—
Else his design will fail—to keep them living.

[He sings in Gonzalo's ear]

While you snore beside this sea,
　Open-eyed conspiracy　　　　　　295
　　Now sees its break.
　If for life you have a care,
Shake off slumber and beware.
　　Awake, awake!

ANTONIO
Then let us both act quickly.　　　　　　300

[Antonio and Sebastian draw their swords]

GONZALO
[waking] Now, good angels protect the King!

[The others wake up]

ALONSO
What's this?—Wake up!—Why have you drawn your
　swords?
Why are you filled with terror?

GONZALO
　　　　　　What's the matter?

SEBASTIAN
While standing watch here during your repose,
Just now, we heard an eerie burst of bellowing   305
Like bulls, or maybe lions. It did not wake you?
A terrifying sound.

ALONSO
                    But I heard nothing.

ANTONIO
And loud enough to jolt a monster's ear,
To cause the earth to shake! No doubt the roar
Of a whole herd of lions.

ALONSO
                    You heard this, Gonzalo?   310

GONZALO
Upon my honor, sir, I heard some humming,
Strange humming, I might add, which woke me up.
I shook you, sir, and yelled. As my eyes opened,
I saw their weapons drawn. There was a noise,
That's certain. We had better be on guard   315
Or leave this place at once. Let's draw our weapons.

ALONSO
Lead us from here, and let's expand our search
For my poor son.

GONZALO
                    Heaven save him from these beasts!
He must be on this island.

ALONSO
                    Lead us on.

ARIEL
Prospero my lord shall hear what I have done.   320
So, King, go safely on to seek your son.

                    [They exit]

Scene Two. Another Part of the Island

[Enter CALIBAN, with a load of wood]
[The sound of thunder is heard]

CALIBAN
May all contagion that the sun sucks up
From bogs, fens, swamps, plague Prospero and inch
By inch devour him! [thunder] His demons hear me,
And yet I'm forced to curse. But they won't jab,
Scare me with spiny goblins, chuck me in   5
The mire, or lead me with a jack-o'-lantern
Through darkness off the path, unless he says so,
But with each little thing, they set upon me,
Sometimes like apes that sneer at me and chatter
Before they bite, and then like hedgehogs that   10
Will roll beneath my shoeless feet and raise
Their quills at every step. And sometimes I'm
Entwined by adders, who with forking tongues
Will hiss 'til I've gone mad.

[Enter TRINCULO]

                              Look here now, lo!
Here comes one of his spirits to torment me   15
For bringing wood back slowly. I'll lie flat.
Perhaps he will not notice me.

TRINCULO (a jester and Alonso's servant)
There's not a single bush or shrub to fend off wind and
weather, and another storm is brewing. I hear it singing in
the wind. That black cloud there, that huge one—it looks   20
like some rotten barrel that's ready to dump its liquor. If
it thunders like the one before, I don't know where I'll hide
my head. That cloud cannot help but drop it by the pail-
ful. What have we here? A man or a fish? Dead or alive? A
fish, he smells like a fish—an ancient one, not the freshest   25
piece of mackerel. A strange fish! Were I in England now,
as once I was, and stuck this fish in a sideshow, there's

not a fool on holiday who wouldn't pay a piece of silver to
see it. A man would make a fortune off this monster there.
Any strange creature can bring one. They will not give a   30
farthing to help a crippled beggar but will lay out ten to
see a dead Indian. Legs like a man, and fins like arms!
It's warm. Well I'll be! So much for that opinion; it's mine
no longer. This is no fish; it's an islander who has recently
been the victim of a thunderbolt. [thunder] Oh no, another   35
storm is coming. My best chance is to crawl under his cloak.
There is no other shelter hereabouts. Misery acquaints a
man with strange bed-fellows. I'll take cover here till the
dregs of this storm have passed.

[Enter STEPHANO singing, with a bottle in his hand]

STEPHANO (Alonso's butler)
      [sings] *I'll go no more to sea, to sea,*   40
       Here shall I die ashore—

That's a very scurvy tune to sing at a man's funeral. Well,
here's what gives me comfort. [drinks]

  [sings] *The master, the swabber, the boatswain, and me,*
       The gunner, and his mate,   45
   Loved Mall, Meg, and Marian, and Margery,
       But none of us cared for Kate.
     For she had a tongue with a tang,
     Would cry to a sailor "Go hang!"
    She loved not the odor of tar nor of pitch,   50
 Yet her tailor could scratch her if she had an itch.
    Then to sea, boys, and let her go hang!

This is a scurvy tune too. But this gives me comfort. [drinks]

CALIBAN
Do not torment me. O!

STEPHANO
What's going on? Are there devils here? Do you play tricks   55
on us with savages and men from the Indies? Ha! I have

not escaped drowning to now fear your four legs, for it has
been said, "As perfect a man as ever walked on four legs
cannot make him give ground." And they'll keep saying it
as long as Stephano breathes through his nostrils.   60

CALIBAN
This demon's tormenting me. O!

STEPHANO
Some monster's inhabiting the isle—with four legs—who
seems to shake with fever. How the devil did he learn our
language? For that alone he'll get some aid from me. If I can
cure him and keep him tame and get him to Naples, he's a   65
present for any emperor who's ever had leather in his shoes.

CALIBAN
Do not torment me, I beg you. I'll bring my wood home faster.

STEPHANO
He's having fits now and not making much sense. I'll give
him a sip from my bottle. If he has never drunk wine before, it will go a long way toward stopping these fits. If I   70
can cure him and keep him tame, there's no price I can't
ask. Whoever wants him will have to pay, and then some.

CALIBAN
You haven't hurt me much yet, but it is coming. I can tell
from your shaking. Prospero is working on you.

STEPHANO
Come on now. Open your mouth. Here's something that   75
could get a cat talking. Open your mouth. This will shake
off your shaking, I can tell you, and then some.

[Pours wine in CALIBAN'S mouth. He does not like it]

You don't know a friend when you see one. Open your trap
again.

TRINCULO
I know that voice. It has to be—but he has drowned, and   80
these are devils. O, save me!

STEPHANO
Four legs and two voices— such an exquisite monster! His
front end, now, speaks well of his friend. His back end ut-
ters ugly words and derision. If it takes all the wine in my
bottle to cure him, I will treat this fever. Come on.   85

[CALIBAN drinks]

That's enough! I will pour some in your other mouth.

TRINCULO
Stephano!

STEPHANO
Did your other mouth call my name? Mercy, mercy! A devil,
not a monster. I'm spoonless, and you need a long one to
eat with the devil.   90

TRINCULO
Stephano! If you are Stephano, touch me and speak to
me, for I am Trinculo—don't be afraid—your good friend
Trinculo.

STEPHANO
If you are Trinculo, come out. I'll pull you by the smaller
legs. If any of these are Trinculo's legs, it's these. You are   95
Trinculo indeed! How did you come to be the excrement of
this mooncalf? Can he expel Trinculos?

TRINCULO
I thought he'd been killed by a thunderstroke. But didn't
you drown, Stephano? I hope you haven't drowned. Has the
storm blown over? I hid myself under the dead mooncalf's   100
shroud out of fear of the storm. And are you alive, Stephano?
O Stephano, two Neapolitans survived!

[Embraces STEPHANO and dances around]

STEPHANO
Please, do not spin me around. My stomach is unsettled.

CALIBAN
[aside] These are fine creatures if they are not sprites. This
one's a splendid god who brings celestial liquor. I will kneel   105
before him.

STEPHANO
How did you survive? How'd you get here? Swear on this
bottle and tell me how you got here?—I escaped on a barrel
of sweet wine, which the sailors heaved overboard—I swear
it upon this bottle, which I made from the bark of a tree   110
with my own hands after I was cast ashore.

CALIBAN
I'll swear upon that bottle that I'm your loyal subject, for
the liquor is not of this earth.

STEPHANO
[ignores Caliban] Here. [hands Trinculo the bottle] Swear
on it and tell how you survived.   115

TRINCULO
[drinks and hands the bottle back] Swam ashore, man, like
a duck. I can swim like a duck. I swear it.

STEPHANO
[passing the bottle] Here, kiss the book again. Though you
can swim like a duck, you drink like a goose.

TRINCULO
O Stephano, do you have any more of this?   120

STEPHANO
The whole barrel, man. My cellar is in a rock by the seaside,
where my wine is hidden. [to Caliban] Ah, mooncalf! How
is your fever doing?

CALIBAN
Didn't you drop from heaven?

STEPHANO
Right off the moon, I assure you. I was the Man-in-the-Moon   125
once upon a time.

CALIBAN
I have seen you in her, and I do revere you. My mistress
showed you to me, and your dog, and your bundle of sticks.

STEPHANO
Come. Swear by this. Kiss the book. I will replenish it soon
with new contents. Swear by this.   130

[CALIBAN drinks]

TRINCULO
In better light, this isn't much of a monster! Me afraid
of him? A very weak monster! The Man-in-the-Moon? A
wretched, gullible monster! That's quite a swig, monster.
That's the truth!

CALIBAN
I'll show you every fertile inch o' the island and will kiss   135
your foot. I hope you'll be my god.

TRINCULO
In the light of day, an underhanded and drunken monster.
When his god's asleep, he'll steal his bottle.

CALIBAN
I'll kiss your foot. I'll swear to be your subject.

STEPHANO
Come on, then. Get down and swear it.   140

TRINCULO
I will die laughing at this puppy-headed monster. What a
scurvy monster. I'd have a mind to beat him—

STEPHANO
Come, kiss them.

TRINCULO
If the poor monster wasn't drunk. An abominable monster.

CALIBAN
I'll show you the best springs. I'll pick you berries.   145
I'll fish for you and get you ample wood.
A plague upon the tyrant that I serve!
I'll bring him no more sticks. I'll follow you,
You wondrous man.

TRINCULO
What a ridiculous monster, to turn a poor drunkard into   150
a marvel.

CALIBAN
Please, let me show you where the apples[5] grow.
With my long nails, I'll dig up earth-nuts for you,
Show you a jay's nest, teach you how to snare
The nimble marmoset. I'll show you clusters   155
Of hazelnuts, and when I can, I'll get you
Young mussels[6] from the rocks. Will you go with me?

STEPHANO
Please lead the way with no more talking. Trinculo, with
the King and the rest of our company drowned, we'll take
possession here. [to Caliban] Here, carry my bottle. Trin- 160
culo, my fellow, we'll soon fill it up again.

CALIBAN
[sings drunkenly] Farewell, master. Farewell, farewell!

TRINCULO
A howling monster, a drunken monster.

CALIBAN
     [sings] *No more dams I'll make for fish,*
         No wood for fires   165

As he requires,
Won't scrape a plate nor wash a dish.
'Ban 'Ban, Ca-Caliban,
Has a new master—You'll need a new man.

Freedom, celebration day! Celebration day, freedom! Free- 170
dom, celebration, freedom!

STEPHANO
O splendid monster! Lead the way.

[Exit]

The Tempest

Act Three

Act Three

Scene One. The Island

[Enter FERDINAND, carrying a log]

FERDINAND (King Alonso's son)
Some sports are painful, but the effort spent
Won't cancel the delight.[1] Some lowly chores
Are done quite nobly, and the poorest tasks
Look toward rich outcomes. Menial work
Should be both tedious and repugnant, yet   5
The mistress that I serve brings life to what
Is dead and makes work pleasure. Her gentleness
Is ten times greater than her father's crossness,
And he is made of harshness. I'm forced to move
Logs by the thousands, piling them up here   10
By his strict orders. My sweet mistress weeps
To see me work and says that tasks this base
Are never done by ones like me. I drift,
But these sweet thoughts add vigor to my efforts.
I'm busiest when I have them.[2]

[Enter MIRANDA. PROSPERO follows
at a distance, unseen]

MIRANDA
                          Please, poor thing,   15
Don't work so hard. I wish the lightning had
Burned up these logs he ordered you to pile.
Please, set it down and rest now. When these burn,
They'll weep for having tired you so. My father
Is deep in study. Please now, rest yourself.   20
He's occupied for three more hours.

79

FERDINAND
Dear mistress,
The sun will set before I will fulfill
What I must toil to do.

MIRANDA
If you'll sit down,
I'll move them for a while. Give me that log.
I'll carry it to the pile.

FERDINAND
No, precious creature,   25
I'd rather tear my muscles, break my back,
Than have you undertake such shameful work
While I sit idly by.

MIRANDA
It suits me just
As well as it does you, and I might do it
With much less strain for unlike you it's not   30
Against my will.

PROSPERO
[aside] Poor bug, you are infected!
This visit shows it clearly.

MIRANDA
You look weary.

FERDINAND
No, noble mistress, I'd be fresh as morning
With you nearby at night. And may I ask,
Mainly so I can put it in my prayers,   35
What is your name?

MIRANDA
Miranda.—O I said it,
I broke my father's order!

FERDINAND
                    Miranda! Wonder!
Indeed, she's wonder's highest mark, worth what's
Most valued in the world! So many a lady
I've eyed with high regard, and many a time   40
Their pleasing tongues have made a slave of my
Attentive ear. For various qualities
Have I liked various women, but not one
This fully in my soul, for some defect
In each would challenge her best attribute   45
And fight it to a draw. But you, O you,
So perfect and so peerless, are created
From every creature's best.

MIRANDA
                         I've never known
One from my sex, nor viewed a woman's face
Except mine in a mirror. Nor have I seen   50
More of what are called men than you, good friend,
And my dear father. Faces from beyond

This isle I'm ignorant of, but I would stake
My chastity, my dowry's jewel, that I
Would want no other partner in this world   55
And can't imagine any form, besides
Yourself, that I would like. But I am rambling
A bit too wildly and forgetting to
Obey my father's rules.

FERDINAND
                        I am, in rank,
A prince, Miranda, and I think, a king—   60
I wish I weren't!—and would no more allow
Myself to be this timber slave than I'd
Let flies breed in my mouth. Hear my soul speak:
The instant I first saw you, my heart flew
To pledge itself to you and to reside   65
Where it can be your slave. It's for your sake
That I'm this tireless log-man.

MIRANDA
                        Do you love me?

FERDINAND
O heaven, O earth, bear witness to these sounds
And crown what I have vowed with good results
If I speak truly! If these words are hollow,   70
Turn my best hopes to something evil. I,
Beyond whatever limits this world knows,
Love, prize, and honor you.

MIRANDA
                        I am a fool
To weep when I am glad.

PROSPERO
                        [aside] Good luck to have
Such natures meet! May heaven's grace rain down   75
On what develops here!

FERDINAND
                        Why are you weeping?

MIRANDA
At my unworthiness, afraid to offer
What I desire to give and even more
To reach what I would die for. Foolish talk—
The more it seeks to hide itself, the more   80
The bulge will show. Be gone, pretended shyness,
And guide me, pure and honest innocence.
I am your wife if you will marry me.
If not, I'll die your maid. To be your spouse,
You may deny me that, but I will be,   85
Wish it or not, your servant.

FERDINAND
[kneels] And I'll be yours, dear mistress, forever humble.

MIRANDA
My husband, then?

FERDINAND
                 And one whose heart desires it
As much as slaves do freedom. Here's my hand.

MIRANDA
And mine, with my heart in it. And now farewell   90
For one half hour.

FERDINAND
                 A million more farewells.

[Exit FERDINAND and MIRANDA separately]

PROSPERO
As thrilled as they are with this I can't be,
For they are quite surprised, yet nothing could
Make me rejoice like this. I'll get my book
Because before our supper time, there's much   95
Related business I must tend to.

[Exit]

Scene Two. Another Part of the Island

[Enter CALIBAN, STEPHANO, and TRINCULO]

STEPHANO
You don't need to tell me. When the cask is empty, we will
drink water but not one drop before. So tie up and come on
board. Servant-monster, a drink on me.

TRINCULO
Servant-monster? An island of freaks and fools![3] They say
there's only five upon this isle. We are three of them. If   5
the other two have brains like ours, the state is tottering.

STEPHANO
Drink, servant-monster, when I tell you to. Your eyes are
setting in your head.

TRINCULO
Where else could they set? He'd be a fine monster indeed,
if they were setting in his tail.   10

STEPHANO
My man-monster has drowned his tongue in vino. As for me,
the sea cannot drown me. I swam, before I reached the shore,
five and thirty leagues, more or less. By this light above,
you shall be my lieutenant, monster, or my flag-bearer.

TRINCULO
Your lieutenant, if you please. He's already flagging.   15

STEPHANO
We won't retreat, Monsieur Monster.

TRINCULO
Nor advance either. You'll lie like dogs, yet never say a thing.

STEPHANO
Mooncalf, speak once in your life if you're a good mooncalf.

CALIBAN
How is your honor? Let me lick your shoe. I won't serve
him. He is not valiant.   20

TRINCULO
You lie, you ignorant monster. I'm ready to wrestle a
constable. Why, you depraved fish, you. Was ever a man
a coward who has drunk as much grape as I have today?
How can a monster who's half fish tell such a monstrous lie?

CALIBAN
Lo, how he mocks me! Will you let him, my lord?   25

TRINCULO
"Lord," he says! That a monster could be such a natural-
born fool!

CALIBAN
Lo, lo again! Bite him to death, I beg you.

STEPHANO
Trinculo, watch that tongue of yours. If you're thinking
mutiny—the next tree's your gallows! The poor monster's   30
my subject and must receive the appropriate respect.

CALIBAN
I thank my noble lord. If it pleases you, will you once again
hear my petition to you?

STEPHANO
Indeed I will. Kneel and repeat it. I will stand, and so shall
Trinculo.   35

[Enter ARIEL, invisible]

CALIBAN
As I told you before, I'm ruled by a usurper, a sorcerer, who
through cunning has robbed me of this island.

ARIEL
[as if Trinculo] You lie.

CALIBAN
[to Trinculo] You lie, you jesting monkey, you.
I wish my valiant master would destroy you.   40
I do not lie.

STEPHANO
Trinculo, if you interrupt his tale again, with this hand I
will displace some of your teeth.

TRINCULO
But I didn't say anything.

STEPHANO
Quiet, then, and no more. Proceed.   45

CALIBAN
I say, through sorcery he got this isle.
From me he got it. If your greatness will
Retaliate for me—I know you'd dare it,
Though this thing wouldn't [indicating Trinculo]—

STEPHANO
That's quite certain.   50

CALIBAN
You'll be the lord of it, and I'll serve you.

STEPHANO
How would this be accomplished? Can you take me to the
party involved?

CALIBAN
Yes, yes, my lord. I'll show you where he sleeps,
And you can pound a nail into his head.   55

ARIEL
You're lying. You can't do that.

CALIBAN
You motley ninny. What a scurvy clown!
I must beseech your greatness, give him blows
And take his bottle from him. When that's gone,
He will be down to brine, for I won't show him   60
Where the fresh springs are.

STEPHANO
Trinculo, it's dangerous to push this further. Interrupt the
monster with one word more, and with this hand, I'll toss
all mercy out the door and make fish stock out of you.

TRINCULO
Why, what did I do? I did nothing. I'll move farther away.   65

STEPHANO
Didn't you say he's lying?

ARIEL
You're lying.

STEPHANO
Do I now? Take that. [slaps Trinculo] There's more of this
if you call me a liar again.

TRINCULO
I did not call you a liar. Both your mind and hearing gone?   70
A pox on your bottle! That's what wine and drinking do. A
plague on your monster, and the devil take those hands of
yours!

CALIBAN
Ha, ha, ha!

STEPHANO
Now, go on with your tale.—[to Trinculo] Please, stand   75
farther over there.⁴

CALIBAN
Beat him some more. After a little more, I'll beat him too.

STEPHANO
[to Trinculo] Farther over. [to Caliban] Come, proceed.

CALIBAN
Why, as I told you, in the afternoon
He usually takes a nap. Then you can brain him,   80
After you've seized his books, or with a log
Batter his skull, or skewer him with a stake,
Or cut his windpipe with your knife. Remember:
First seize his books. Without them he's a dolt
Like me and doesn't have one spirit that   85
He can command. As much as I, they hate him
Down to the roots. Be sure to burn his books.
He has some fine effects—he calls them that—
To decorate a house he hopes to have.
The thing most deeply to consider is   90
The beauty of his daughter. He himself
Says she's without a peer. I've seen no women
Besides her and my mother Sycorax,
But she surpasses Sycorax more than
The greatest does the least.   95

STEPHANO
Is she that splendid a lass?

CALIBAN
I guarantee she'll make your bed look good
And bear a splendid brood for you.

STEPHANO
Monster, I will kill this man. His daughter and I will be
King and Queen—God save us—and Trinculo and you shall   100
be my viceroys. Do you like the plan, Trinculo?

TRINCULO
Excellent.

STEPHANO
Give me your hand. I am sorry I beat you, but while you
live, watch that tongue of yours.

CALIBAN
In half an hour, he will be asleep.   105
Will you destroy him then?

STEPHANO
                    Ay, on my honor.

ARIEL
[aside] This I will tell my master.

CALIBAN
You've cheered me up. I'm full of pleasure now.
Let us be merry. Will you belt out the round
That you just taught me?   110

STEPHANO
Any reasonable request, monster, anything reasonable.
Come on, Trinculo, let us sing.

            [sings] *Sneer at 'em, jeer at 'em,*
                Jeer at 'em, sneer at 'em;
                I'll think what I please.   115

CALIBAN
That's not the tune.

        [ARIEL plays the tune on a tabor (a small drum)
                    and a pipe]

STEPHANO
What's this echo?

TRINCULO
That's the round's melody, played by the Man Who Was
Nobody.

STEPHANO
If you are human, then show yourself in that form. If you   120
are a devil, well, it's your call.

TRINCULO
O, forgive me my sins!

STEPHANO
He who dies pays all debts. I defy you! Mercy upon us!

CALIBAN
Are you afraid?

STEPHANO
No, monster, not I.   125

CALIBAN
Be not afraid. The isle is full of noises,
Sounds, and sweet tunes that give delight and hurt not.
Sometimes a thousand strumming instruments
Will hum around my ears, and sometimes voices,
Though I have just awoken from long sleep,   130
Will make me sleep again, and in my dreams
The clouds will open up and drop on me
Such riches that when I awake, I cry
And beg to dream again.

STEPHANO
This is turning into a splendid kingdom, where music fills   135
my court for free.

CALIBAN
When Prospero is destroyed.

STEPHANO
That will happen soon. I heard your story.

TRINCULO
The sound is moving away. Let's follow it, and afterwards
we'll do our work.   140

STEPHANO
Lead, monster. We'll follow. I wish I could see this tabor-
player. He's really banging on it.

TRINCULO
You coming? I'll follow you, Stephano.

[Exit]

Scene Three. In a Maze on the Island

[Enter ALONSO, SEBASTIAN, ANTONIO, GONZALO,
    ADRIAN, FRANCISCO, and others]

GONZALO
O Mary, I can go no further, sir.
My old bones ache. Stuck in a maze, indeed,
With straightaways and curlycues. Be kind
And let me rest.

ALONSO
              Old lord, I can't find fault
With you. Exhaustion has attached a lien   5
To me and flagged my spirit. Sit and rest.
Right here I'll now dispose of hope and keep
Up this deceit no longer. He's drowned,
This one we've roamed to find, and the sea mocks
Our fruitless search on land. Let's call it off.   10

ANTONIO
[draws Sebastian aside] I'm truly glad that he's run out
    of hope.
Don't let one setback lure you from the act
You've vowed to carry out.

SEBASTIAN
          [aside to Antonio] We'll take advantage
Of any opening.

ANTONIO
          [aside to Sebastian] Let it be tonight.
For now that they're fatigued by travel, they   15

Will not and can't maintain the vigilance
They did when fresh.

SEBASTIAN
                    [aside to Antonio] I say, tonight. It's set.

[Strange and solemn music. PROSPERO enters
and is perched above them, invisible.]⁵

ALONSO
What is this chorus? Listen my good friends.

GONZALO
Marvellous, sweet music!

[Enter several strange BEINGS, bringing in sumptu-
ous food and drink. They dance around it with gentle
gestures of greeting. They invite King ALONSO and the
others to eat, then depart.]

ALONSO
They're kind protectors. Heavens! What was that?   20

SEBASTIAN
A living puppet show. From now on I'll
Believe in unicorns, that in Arabia,
A single phoenix rising from its ashes
Is reigning there right now.

ANTONIO
                         Both I believe.
And tall tales needing proof? Bring them to me.   25
I'll swear they're true, and travelers never lie,
Though fools at home disparage 'em.

GONZALO
                         In Naples
If I reported this, would they believe me?
Would they believe I saw such islanders—
For no doubt these are people of the island—   30
Who though they take a monstrous shape, display

A manner that's more courteous than what
You'll find among the human race where few
If any show this.

PROSPERO
    [aside] Honorable lord,
Your words are true, for some of you right here   35
Are worse than devils.

ALONSO
      I can't help but marvel
At how such shapes, such gestures, and such sounds
Although they lack a tongue, are capable
Of mute, superb expression.

PROSPERO
      [aside] Hold your praise.

FRANCISCO
Strange how they vanished.   40

SEBASTIAN
What does it matter?
They left their dinner here, and we have stomachs.
You want a taste of what is here?

ALONSO
      Not I.

GONZALO
Truly, sir, do not fear. When we were boys,
Who would believe that there were mountain folk 45
With necks that sag like bulls, whose throats were draped
With folds of flesh? Or that the world had men
Whose heads were in their breasts? Each traveler now
Who makes it home against all odds assures
Us that it's true.

ALONSO
    I'm going to eat. This meal   50

May be my last, but what is there to lose?
The best is past. Brother, my lord the Duke,
Step up and join us.

[Thunder and lightning]
[Enter ARIEL, in the guise of a harpy (a woman with
wings and talons). He claps his wings upon the
table and makes the banquet disappear]

ARIEL
You are three men of sin, and Destiny,
Whose instrument is all that lies beneath   55
The moon, has caused the always-hungry sea
To belch you up and place you on this island
Where no men dwell—yes, you who count among
Men most unfit to live, I've made you crack,
And valor of this type can make men hang   60
And drown themselves.

[ALONSO, SEBASTIAN, and others draw their swords]

                            You fools! I and my partners
Are agents sent by Fate. The elements
Your swords are forged from could as easily wound
The roaring wind or kill with mocked-at stabs
The always-healing water as diminish   65
One fiber in my plume. My fellow agents,
They likewise are invulnerable. Your swords,
If they could hurt us, are too heavy now
For you to lift them. But remember this—
And that's what brings me here —you three displaced   70
Good Prospero from Mílan, and exposed
Him to the sea, him and his innocent child,
An awful deed the powers—delaying, not
Forgetting—have avenged by firing up
The seas and shores and, yes, all of creation   75
Against your peace of mind. Alonso, they've
Deprived you of a son. [to all three] And I pronounce
A ruin so prolonged—no quicker death's

This bad—that it will dog you step by step
With no protection from the wrath it drops   80
In this so desolate isle upon your heads
Except what sorrow in your hearts may bring
And blameless living from now on.

[ARIEL vanishes in thunder]
[Then to soft music, the SHAPES re-enter and dance,
mocking and grimacing, and carrying out the table]

PROSPERO
You have portrayed this harpy splendidly,
My Ariel, with grace as it devoured.   85
From my instructions you omitted nothing
You were to say. Likewise, the other spirits
Showed energy and marvelous detail
In each role played. The highest of my spells
Have worked and left my enemies tied up   90
For now by madness. Now they're in my power.
Hysterical I'll leave them, while I visit
Young Ferdinand, who they assume has drowned,
And his and my belovèd darling.

[Exit above]

GONZALO
By all that's holy, sir, why do you stand   95
And stare in horror?

ALONSO
                    Oh, it's monstrous, monstrous!
The towering waves appeared to speak of it,
The winds to sing it to me, and the thunder,
That deep and dreadful organ-pipe, pronounced
The name of Prospero, adding bass notes to   100
My sins. For that, my son must rest in muck
And I will seek and lie with him in mud
As deep as any ever plumbed.

[Exit ALONSO]

SEBASTIAN
If they come one fiend at a time,
I'll fight a legion of them.

ANTONIO
      I'm right behind you.   105

   [Exit SEBASTIAN and ANTONIO]

GONZALO
All three of them are desperate. Their great guilt,
Like poison that will build up over time,
Is nibbling at their strength. So if you would,
Since you have suppler limbs, follow them swiftly,
And hinder what this mania in them   110
May now provoke.

ADRIAN
     Please follow after me.

     [Exit]

The Tempest

Act Four

Act Four

Scene One. Outside Prospero's Lodge

[Enter PROSPERO, FERDINAND, and MIRANDA]

PROSPERO
[to Ferdinand] If I have too severely punished you,
In compensation for your suffering,
I've offered you a third of my own life,
The one for whom I've lived, and once again
I offer you her hand. All your vexations   5
Were merely trials of your love, and you
Withstood them admirably. Here, under heaven,
I now confirm it, my rich gift. O Ferdinand!
Don't smile at me for boasting of her so.
You'll find that she outruns all praise and leaves   10
It limping far behind.

FERDINAND
                    An oracle
Could not convince me otherwise.

PROSPERO
Then, as my gift, an acquisition you
Have earned so worthily, take my daughter. But
If you untie her virgin-knot before   15
All sacred ceremonies are performed
Or holy rites can be administered,
The heavens will not let its sweet dew fall
To make this union grow, but barren hate,
Sour-eyed contempt, and conflict will be strewn   20
Across your marriage bed, with weeds so loathsome

99

You both will hate it. So take heed, as Hymen,
The god of marriage, lights his lamp.

FERDINAND
                                    I hope
For quiet days, fine offspring, and long life,
With love that is so strong, the hidden lair,   25
The opportune locale, the worst temptation,
Our spirit's darker side, could never melt
My honor into lust and mar the day
Of celebration, one so long I'll think
The Sun God's steeds have stopped dead in their tracks   30
And Night's in chains below.

PROSPERO
                        Well said.
Sit, then, and talk with her. She's now your own.
Here, Ariel! My industrious servant, Ariel!

[Enter ARIEL]

ARIEL
I'm here. What does my potent master wish?

PROSPERO
You and your underlings, on your last mission   35
Were quite impressive, and I need from you
Another trick like that. Go bring that rabble,
Whom I've put in your power, here to this place.
Induce them to move quickly, for I must
Bestow upon the eyes of this young couple   40
A snippet of my magic. It's my promise,
And they're expecting it.

ARIEL
                        Immediately?

PROSPERO
Yes, in a wink.

ARIEL
Before you can say "come" and "'go,"
And breathe twice, and cry "so, so,"   45
Each one, dancing on his toe,
Will be here with his smile aglow.
Do you love me, master? No?

PROSPERO
Dearly, my graceful Ariel. Do not approach
Until you hear me call.

ARIEL
                         Fine. Understood.   50

                    [Exit]

PROSPERO
[to Ferdinand] You gave your word. Don't give this flirting
    too
Much rein. The strongest oaths go up like straw
When fire is in your blood. Be more restrained
Or so much for your vow!

FERDINAND
                    [holding Miranda] I promise, sir,
This chaste, white snow that leans against my heart   55
Abates the passion in my liver.[1]

PROSPERO
                    Well.—
Come on, my Ariel. Better one sprite extra
Than one too few. Appear and do it promptly.

                [Soft music]

No tongues! Just eyes! Be silent.

            [Enter IRIS, messenger of the gods,
                a rainbow above her]

The Wedding Masque

IRIS (a spirit)
Ceres, most bounteous one, your yields so high   60
Of wheat, oats, barley, fodder, peas, and rye;
Your grassy mountains, home to nibbling sheep,
And meadows thatched with winter hay so deep;
Your levies so entwined with florae thick,[2]
Which sodden April at your call will pick   65
To make chaste nymphs a crown; your witchy shrubs,
Whose shadows a rejected bachelor loves,
His lass now vanished; and your well-pruned hedge;
Your sea shore and its sterile, rocky edge,
Where you take air—the Queen who rules the sky,   70
Whose rainbow arch and messenger am I,
Says leave all this and join her sovereign grace,
Here on this grassy spot, this very place,
To sport with her. How swift her peacocks fly.

[JUNO, wife of Jupiter, descends in a chariot
drawn by peacocks]

Approach, rich Ceres, greet her—that is why.   75

[Enter CERES]

CERES (a spirit)
Hail, rainbowed messenger, who to this day,
The wife of Jupiter you will obey,
Who, with your saffron wings, upon my flowers
Disperses honey and refreshing showers;
Whose multi-colored arch crowns and sustains   80
My brush-filled acres and my rolling plains,
A rich scarf for proud earth—why has your Queen
Summoned me here to this well-tended green?

IRIS
To celebrate a contract of true love
And to this blessèd pair make a gift of   85
Some of your wealth.

CERES
Do you know, rainbowed one,
If Venus has with Cupid, her blind son,
Accompanied the Queen. That scandalous pair
And Pluto schemed to take my daughter where
She's in the underworld six months each year,   90
So I've forsworn them.

IRIS
You don't need to fear
Her company. Her "godliness" I hear
Drawn by her doves, cut clouds to find her way
To Cyprus with her son. The two, they say,
Placed spells designed to tempt this man and maid,   95
Whose vows are that no right to bed be paid
Till Hymen's torch is lighted. All in vain.
Mars's lustful darling has gone home again;
Her waspish, stinging son has broke his arrows,
Swears he will shoot no more, just play with sparrows,   100
And simply be a boy.

[JUNO descends]

CERES
The Queen so high,
Great Juno, comes. Her gait we know her by.

JUNO (a spirit)
How is my bounteous sister? Go with me
To bless this union, prosperous they will be
And honored by their offspring.   105

[They sing]

JUNO
[sings] *Honor, riches, marriage-blessing,*
Long continuance, and increasing,
Hourly joys remain upon you!
Juno sings her blessings on you.

CERES

[sings] *Earth's increase, abundance plenty,*   110
    Barns and granaries never empty;
    Vines from clustering bunches bending,
    Plants with goodly yields unending;
    Fall continues on to Spring,
    Unceasing harvest it will bring!   115
    Scarcity and want will shun you,
    For Ceres' blessing is upon you.

FERDINAND
A vision that is quite majestic and
Enchantingly harmonious. Am I too bold
To think they're spirits?

PROSPERO
                Spirits called up from   120
Their native confines by my art to serve
My current fancies.

FERDINAND
             Let me live here always.
A wise and wondrous father, and so rare,³
Makes this a Paradise.

        [JUNO and CERES whisper to each other
        and then send IRIS to perform a task]

PROSPERO
             Dear one, be silent.⁴
Juno's and Ceres' whispering is important.   125
There's more to do here. Hush and make no sound,
Or else the magic's ruined.

IRIS
You nymphs, you naiads, of the winding brooks,
With crowns of grass and always innocent looks,
Leave your swift channels and on this green land   130
Answer your summons. Juno will command.
Come, you chaste nymphs, and help to celebrate
A contract of true love. Don't be too late.

[Enter NYMPHS]

You weary reapers, burnt by August sun
Come up here from the furrows, join our fun;   135
Take this day off; a straw hat you will wear
And with each fresh, young nymph you'll make a pair
And join a country dance.

[Enter REAPERS, appropriately dressed. They join with
   the NYMPHS in a graceful dance, towards the end of
   which PROSPERO starts up suddenly and speaks]

PROSPERO
[aside] The foul conspiracy had slipped my mind
That the beast Caliban and his confederates   140
Have made against my life. The time to launch
Their plot is near. [to the Spirits] Well done. Depart. No
   more!

[A strange, hollow, and chaotic noise is heard,
   and the disappointed spirits vanish][5]

FERDINAND
This is strange. Some emotion in your father
Has stirred him greatly.

MIRANDA
                        I've never till this day
Seen anger touch him with such turbulence.   145

PROSPERO
You mood has changed, my son, and seems disturbed,
As if you are dismayed. Be cheerful, sir.
Our revels now are finished. All these actors,
As I explained before, were spirits and
Have melted into air, into thin air;   150
And like the hollow framework of this spectacle,
The cloud-capped towers, the gorgeous palaces,
The solemn temples, the great globe itself,
Yes, all who dwell within it shall dissolve,

And like this flimsy pageant, once it's faded,   155
Leave not a wisp behind. We are such stuff
As dreams are made of and our little life
Is rounded off by sleep. Sir, I am vexed.
Bear with my weakness. My old brain is troubled.
Don't be disturbed by my infirmity.   160
If you desire, withdraw into my lodge
And rest yourself. I'll walk around a bit
To calm my pulsing mind.

FERDINAND, MIRANDA
                     We wish you peace.

[Exit]

[Enter ARIEL]

PROSPERO
I think and you appear. I thank you, Ariel.

ARIEL
Each thought I cling to. What's your pleasure?

PROSPERO
                                    Spirit,   165
We must prepare to challenge Caliban.

ARIEL
Ay, my commander. When I was playing "Ceres,"
I thought that I should tell you of it but
I feared I'd anger you.

PROSPERO
Say once again, where did you leave these rascals?   170

ARIEL
I told you, sir, they were red-hot from drinking,
So full of valor that they slashed the air
For breathing in their faces, beat the ground
Because it kissed their feet, yet they kept on

Towards their objective. Then I beat my tabor, 175
And like unbroken colts, they pricked their ears,
Forced up their eyelids, lifted up their noses
As if they smelled my song, their ears so charmed
That like a calf they tracked my mooing through
Sharp briers, spiked hawthorn, pricking gorse, and thorns, 180
Which punctured their frail shins. I left them in
A filthy scum-laced pond behind your lodge,
To dance up to their chins in muck so foul
You cannot smell their feet.

PROSPERO

Well done, my bird.
We'll have you stay invisible for now. 185
The fripperies in my house, go bring them here
As bait to catch these thieves.

ARIEL

I'll go, I'll go.

[Exit]

PROSPERO
A devil, a born devil, on whose nature
Nurture can never stick; on whom my efforts,
Humanely carried out, were lost, all lost. 190
His body as with age grows uglier,
His mind malignant. I'll torment them all
Until they scream.

[Re-enter ARIEL, carrying glittering apparel
and other items]

Come, hang them on this line.

[PROSPERO and ARIEL remain, invisible]

[Enter CALIBAN, STEPHANO, and TRINCULO,
all wet]

CALIBAN
Please, tread so softly a blind mole won't hear your footsteps.
We're getting near his lodge. 195

STEPHANO
Monster, your fairy, who you say is a harmless fairy, played
more than just a jack or two on us.

TRINCULO
Monster, I reek of horse-piss to the great indignation of
my nose.

STEPHANO
And mine too. Are you listening, monster? If I ever become 200
displeased with you, watch out—

TRINCULO
You'd be one loused-up monster.

CALIBAN
My good lord, keep me always in your favor.
Be patient. You'd wear blinders through all hardship
If you could see the prize. Speak softly, please. 205
It's quiet as midnight here.

TRINCULO
Ay, but to lose our bottles in the pond!

STEPHANO
There is not only disgrace and dishonor in that, monster,
but an infinite loss as well.

TRINCULO
That's worse to me than getting wet. And you still say your 210
fairy's harmless, monster.

STEPHANO
I will fish for my bottle even if the effort puts me in over
my ears.

CALIBAN
Oh, please, my king, be quiet. And look here.
The opening to his lodge. No noise. We'll enter.   215
The good this harm will do is make this island
Forever yours, and I, your Caliban,
Your foot-licker.

STEPHANO
Give me your hand. My thoughts are turning bloody.

TRINCULO
King Stephano! Unequalled! Noble King Stephano. Look   220
at the wardrobe you will have!

CALIBAN
Leave it alone, you fool. It's all just trash.

TRINCULO
O, ho, monster, we know cast-offs when we see them. O
King Stephano!

STEPHANO
Pull down that robe, Trinculo. I swear this hand will have   225
that gown.

TRINCULO
Your Grace shall have it.

CALIBAN
Oh drown this swollen fool! How can you stop
To dote on junk like this? Leave it alone
And do the murder first. If he wakes up,   230
From toe to crown he'll fill our skin with pains
And turn us into something strange.

STEPHANO
Keep quiet, monster. Dear Miss Clothesline, isn't this my
jacket? You have crossed below the line—sailing to warmer
regions where, jacket, you might lose your hair and end   235
up bald.

TRINCULO
Good, good. Stealing crosses the line. How's that one, your
Grace?

STEPHANO
I thank you for that jest. Here, take this garment as payment. Wittiness shall not go unrewarded while I am king   240
of this country. "Stealing crosses the line"—an excellent
mental move. Here's another garment for it.

TRINCULO
Come on, monster. Put some glue on your fingers and grab
the rest.

CALIBAN
I will have none of it. We're wasting time.   245
We'll all be turned to barnacles or apes
With foreheads miserable and low.

STEPHANO
Monster, put your fingers to work. Help us haul this away
to where my hogshead of wine is, or I'll toss you out of my
kingdom. Get going and carry this.   250

TRINCULO
And this.

STEPHANO
Yes, and this.

[The sound of hunters is heard. Enter several SPIRITS,
in the shape of dogs and hounds, tracking the thieves;
PROSPERO and ARIEL sic them on the thieves]

PROSPERO
[to the dogs] Hey, Mountain, hey!

ARIEL
Silver! Sic 'em, Silver!

PROSPERO
Fury, Fury! There, Tyrant, there! Obey!   255

[CALIBAN, STEPHANO, and TRINCULO
are driven off]

Command my demons to afflict their joints
With grinding, tighten up their muscles with

The agèd's cramps, and bruise them till they have
More spots than leopards.

ARIEL

                              Listen to them scream.

PROSPERO
Let them be hunted down. This is the hour   260
When all my enemies lie at my mercy.
My labors soon will end, and then you're free
To roam the air at will. But follow and
Obey a little longer.

[Exit]

The Tempest

Act Five

Act Five

Scene One. Outside Prospero's Lodge

[Enter PROSPERO in his magic robes, and ARIEL]

PROSPERO
My project now is coming to a head,
My spells have held, my spirits obey, and time
Walks tall beneath its load. How late is it?

ARIEL
It's almost six, the time at which, my lord,
You said our work should cease.

PROSPERO
                Indeed I did   5
When I first raised the tempest. Tell me, spirit,
How have the King and his group fared?

ARIEL
                     Confined together
Precisely in the way that you had ordered,
Just as you left them; all prisoners, sir,
In the lime-grove, the windbreak near your lodge.   10
They cannot budge till you release them. Your King,
His brother, and yours too, remain unhinged,
And the remainder mourning over them,
Full to the brim with shock and grief, especially
The one you called "the good old lord," Gonzalo.   15
His tears run down his beard like winter rain
Off thatch. Your spell has worked so well on them
If you beheld them now, your feelings would
Grow tender.

115

PROSPERO
That is what you think, my spirit?

ARIEL
Mine would, sir, were I human.

PROSPERO
Mine must too.   20
Do you, one made of air, have any sense
Of their afflictions, and that I, one of
Their kind, would naturally and keenly share
What they can feel and be more moved than you?
Though their high crimes have pierced my tender core,   25
I've sided in this with my nobler reason
Against my fury. Magnanimity's
More special than revenge. Now that they're penitent,
The sole direction my plan takes should not
Produce another frown. Release them, Ariel.   30
My spells I'll break, their senses I'll restore,
And they shall be themselves.

ARIEL
I'll fetch them, sir.

[Exit]

[Prospero draws a circle with his wand]

PROSPERO
You elves of hills, brooks, tranquil lakes, and groves,
And you who on the sands without a print
Chase Neptune's ebbing sea and flee from him   35
When he comes back; you half-sized puppets who
By moonlight in the grass make sour rings
Where ewes can't graze, whose pastime is to make
The midnight mushroom, who rejoice to hear
The solemn curfew bell, and with whose aid—   40
However weak you agents are—I've dimmed
The noontide sun, raised mutinous winds, and set
Between the green sea and the azure dome

A roaring war. To dreaded rattling thunder
I've given fire and split Jove's stoutest oak   45
With his own bolt, made promontories rock
On their strong base, and plucked up by the roots
The pine and cedar. Graves at my command
Have waked their sleeepers, opened, and released them—
My sorcery's that strong. But this brute magic   50
I now renounce, and after summoning
Some heavenly music—which I'll do right now—

[Prospero waves his wand]

Aimed at the senses of the ones for whom
This tuneful spell is meant, I'll break my wand,
Bury it fathoms deep beneath the ground,   55
And far beneath the depths our tools can plumb
I'll drown my book.

[Solemn music]
[Enter ARIEL, then ALONSO, with lunatic gestures, attended by GONZALO; then SEBASTIAN and ANTONIO,
who behave the same, attended by ADRIAN and FRAN-
CISCO. They all enter the circle that PROSPERO had
made and stand there in a trance. PROSPERO, who is
invisible to them, observes them and speaks]

A solemn tune, the best for comforting
Disturbed imaginings, to cure your brains,
Now useless, boiling in your skull! Stand there,   60
For you're held by a spell.
Holy Gonzalo, honorable man,
My eyes, in sympathy with yours, shed tears
Of fellowship. The spell will soon dissolve
And as the morning sneaks up on the night   65
To melt away the dark, their senses too
Will now disperse the numbing fumes that veil
Their clearing faculties. O good Gonzalo,
Who truly saved me, loyal lord to him
You serve, I will repay in full my debt   70
To you in words and deeds. Such cruelty

You showed, Alonso, toward me and my daughter.
Your brother helped you carry out this act.
Feel torment's pinch, Sebastian. Flesh and blood,
You and my brother, who harbored such ambition,   75
Who tossed aside all pity, who with Sebastian—
Whose inner pinch of torment thus is strongest—
Would here have killed your king, I will forgive you,
Inhuman though you are. Their sense of things
Is on the rise, and the approaching tide   80
Will shortly fill the shoreline of their reason
Which now is foul and muddy. Not one of them
Has yet to see or recognize me. Ariel,
Fetch me my hat and rapier from my lodge.

[Exit ARIEL]

I'll change this costume and present myself   85
As I once did in Mílan. Quickly, spirit
Before long you'll be free.

[ARIEL, on returning, sings and helps to remove
his magician's gown and dress him in clothing
a duke might wear]

ARIEL
[sings] Where the bee sips, so do I;
In a primrose bud I lie;
There I doze when owls do cry.   90
On the bat's back I do fly
Chasing summer merrily.
Merrily, merrily shall I live now
Under the blossom that hangs on the bough.

PROSPERO
Why, that's my fabulous Ariel! I will miss you,   95
But you'll still have your freedom.

[Ariel adusts Prospero's clothing]

Good enough.

To the King's ship, and stay invisible.
There you will find the mariners asleep
Below the deck. The master and the boatswain,
Awaken them and drive them to this spot—   100
Immediately, please.

ARIEL
I'll gulp the air ahead and then return
Before your pulse beats twice.

[Exit ARIEL]

GONZALO
There's torment, trouble, wonder, and amazement—
All these dwell here. Some power from heaven, lead   105
Us from this frightening country!

PROSPERO
                                        Behold, Sir King,
The Duke of Mílan, the wronged Prospero.
For more assurance that a living prince
Is speaking to you now, I will embrace you,
And to you and your company extend   110
A hearty welcome.

ALONSO
                                    You may be who you say
Or some illusion cooked up to delude me,
(And lately that's the case)—who knows? Your pulse,
It beats like flesh and blood, and seeing you,
My mind's distress seems on the mend, and now   115
I fear, a madness held me. This demands—
If real—a quite surprising explanation.
Your dukedom I'll return and pray you'll grant
A pardon for my wrongs. But how did Prospero
Survive and make it here?

PROSPERO
                            [to Gonzalo] First, noble friend,   120
Let me embrace this aging frame, whose honor
Cannot be measured or confined.

GONZALO
                                        I can't
Say if this is or isn't.

PROSPERO
                        The island's taste
Still plays tricks on your tongue and will not let
You trust what's certain. Welcome, my friends all!   125
[aside to Sebastian and Antonio] And as for this fine pair
    of lords, had I
The mind, I'd have his Highness wrap you in
His frown and prove you're traitors, but for now
I'll tell no tales.

SEBASTIAN
                    [aside] The devil's speaking in him.

PROSPERO
No, not a one.   130
You, sir, the wickedest—just calling you
My brother stains my mouth—I will forgive
Your gravest crime, all of them, and demand
My dukedom be restored, your only choice
As things now stand.

ALONSO
                        If you are Prospero,   135
Explain in detail how you could survive
And find us here, who just three hours ago
Were shipwrecked on this shore where I have lost—
How sharp a point the memory of this has—
My dear son Ferdinand.

PROSPERO
                            I'm sorry, sir.   140

ALONSO
Irreparable this loss, beyond what Patience
Herself could ever cure.

PROSPERO
Yet I suspect
You have not sought from her the kindly aid
That's had such great effect when I have had
To bear a similar loss.

ALONSO
What similar loss?   145

PROSPERO
As recent and as great, with fewer means
At hand for me than you may call upon
To deal with such a grievous loss, for I
Have lost my daughter.

ALONSO
A daughter?   150
O heavens, if only they could be in Naples,
A King and Queen! If only it were me
Instead down in that oozing bed of mud
Where my son lies. When did you lose your daughter?

PROSPERO
In this last tempest. I can see these lords   155
Are so amazed at this encounter that
They've swallowed down their reason whole and fear
Their eyes have left their post and words are just
Mere impulse.[1] But however much you have
Been jostled from your senses, know for certain   160
That I am Prospero, the duke tossed out
Of Mílan—yes, that one—who landed by
Surprise upon this shore, where you were shipwrecked,
To be its lord. But that's enough of this.
This chronicle's best told as days go by,   165
Not over breakfast, and it seems improper
At this first meeting. Welcome, sir. This lodge
Here is my court. You'll see I have few servants;
No subjects dwell outside. Please, take a look.
Since you've returned my dukedom to me now,   170
I will repay you with a thing as good,

And at the least bring forth a wonder just
As pleasing as my kingdom.

       [Here PROSPERO reveals FERDINAND and
           MIRANDA, playing chess]

MIRANDA
Sweet lord, you're cheating.

FERDINAND
               No, my dearest love,
I would not for the world.   175

MIRANDA
You might for twenty kingdoms, though, and I'd
Still say you're playing fair.[2]

ALONSO
                If this is just
Another of this island's tricks, I'll lose
My dear son twice.

SEBASTIAN
            Miraculous indeed![3]

FERDINAND
The seas are threatening but merciful.   180
I've cursed them without cause. [kneels]

ALONSO
                   Now all the blessings
Of a glad father circle you! Arise,
And tell us how you got here.

MIRANDA
                 The wonder of it!
How many handsome creatures there are here!
How fine they look! A new and splendid world   185
To have such people in it!

PROSPERO
                    New to you.

ALONSO
Who is this maid with whom you played this game?
You can't have known her for more than three hours.
Is she the goddess that has severed us
And now brings us together?

FERDINAND
                    She's mortal, but   190
Immortal Providence has made her mine.
I chose her when the father who would give
Me guidance was thought lost. She's daughter to
This famous Duke of Mílan, whose renown
I've heard about so many times before   195
But whom I've never seen, from whom I have
Received a second life and second father
As she becomes my lady.

ALONSO
                    And my daughter.
But, O, how oddly it will sound for me
To ask my child for her forgiveness!

PROSPERO
                    Stop, sir.   200
Let's not weigh down our memories with a grief
That now is gone.

GONZALO
                    Inside me, I am weeping,
Or I'd have spoken earlier. Look down, you gods,
And on this couple drop a blessèd crown.
For it is you who chalked the path that brought   205
Us to this place.

ALONSO
                    I say "Amen," Gonzalo!

GONZALO
Was Mílan tossed from Mílan so his heirs
Would be the kings of Naples? O, rejoice
Beyond what's usual. Set this down in gold
On pillars to endure, how in one voyage   210
Your Claribel in Tunis finds a husband,
And Ferdinand, her brother, finds a wife
Where he was stranded; Prospero finds his dukedom
On a poor isle; and we all find ourselves
When no man was himself.

ALONSO
                    [to Ferdinand and Miranda] Give me
    your hands.   215
Let grief and sorrow plague the hearts of those
Who do not wish you joy.

GONZALO
                    So be it. Amen!

[Re-enter ARIEL, with the SHIPMASTER and BOAT-
        SWAIN following in a trance]

O look, sir; look, sir! Here are more of us!
As I foretold, if this land has a gallows,
This fellow will not drown. [to the Boatswain] Your
    blasphemy   220
Threw God's grace overboard, yet not one curse
On shore? No tongue on land? What is the news?

BOATSWAIN
The best news is our King and company
Are safe and sound. And next, our ship—just three
Turns of the hour glass since she broke up—   225
Is caulked and set and rigged as splendidly
As when we put to sea.

ARIEL
                    [aside to Prospero] Sir, all this work
I did while I was gone.

PROSPERO
            [aside to Ariel] Quick-thinking spirit!

ALONSO
These are not natural events. They've moved
From strange to stranger. Tell us how you found us?   230

BOATSWAIN
If I could say that I'd been wide awake, sir,
I'd strive to tell you. We were dead asleep,
And—who knows how—locked up below the deck,
Where we just now by some collection of
Strange noises—roaring, shrieking, jingling chains,   235
And howling, different sounds, all horrible—
Were woken up and straightaway released,
Where we beheld her, trimmed and set to sail,
Our royal, good, and gallant ship, our master
Dancing to see her. Just like that, you see   240
Like in a dream, we're whisked off from the crew
And brought here in a daze.

ARIEL
                  [aside to Prospero] A job well-done?

PROSPERO
[aside to Ariel] Splendid. Such diligence. You shall be free.

ALONSO
As strange a maze as any man has walked in,
And dealings here that go beyond what nature   245
Has ever overseen. Some oracle
Must aid our understanding.

PROSPERO
                  Sir, my lord,
Don't agitate your mind by hammering at
The strangeness of this business. At our leisure—
We'll have some soon—I will alone provide   250
A plausible account of each of these

Events that happened here. Till then be cheerful
And sense the good in this. [aside to Ariel] Come here, my
    spirit.
Set Caliban and his companions free.
Remove the spell.

[Exit ARIEL]

[to Alonso] How are you, gracious sir?   255
Some still are missing from your retinue,
A lad or two that you may have forgotten.

[Re-enter ARIEL, driving in CALIBAN, STEPHANO,
    and TRINCULO, in their stolen apparel]

STEPHANO
It's every man for all the rest, and let no man save himself,
for fate decides it all. *Coraggio*, my splendid monster, have
courage!   260

TRINCULO
If I can trust these lookouts posted in my head, here's a
handsome sight.

CALIBAN
O Setebos, they're splendid spirits indeed!
[seeing Prospero's change of costume] How nice my master's
    dressed! I am afraid
He'll punish me.   265

SEBASTIAN
Ha, ha!
What are these things, my lord Antonio?
Will money buy 'em?

ANTONIO
                        Quite likely. One of them's
No doubt a fish and ready for the market.

PROSPERO
I'd check their crests, my lords. They may not match   270
With those they actually serve. This malformed knave—
His mother was a witch, and one so strong
She could control the moon, cause tides to flow,
And meddle in that realm to stretch its power.[4]
These three have robbed me, and this demi-devil—   275
A mongrel's what he is—has plotted with them
To take my life. Two of these three are ones
You know are yours. This thing of darkness I
Confess is mine.

CALIBAN
                    He'll poke me till I die.

ALONSO
Isn't this Stephano, my drunken butler?   280

SEBASTIAN
He is drunk now. Where did he get wine?

ALONSO
And Trinculo is ripe and reeling. Where'd
They find this marvelous stuff that's made them glow?
How'd you get in this pickle?

TRINCULO
I've been so pickled since I saw you last that I fear it's in   285
my bones for good. No danger of flies laying eggs in me.

SEBASTIAN
Look at you, Stephano!

STEPHANO
Don't touch me. I'm not Stephano. I'm one big cramp.

PROSPERO
Who wished to be king of this island, boy?

STEPHANO
And as oppressive as these pains. 290

ALONSO
[pointing to Caliban] This thing's as strange as any I have
  seen.

PROSPERO
He is as malformed in his character
As in his shape. Go back, boy, to my lodge.
Take your companions. Since you're hoping for
My pardon, decorate it handsomely. 295

CALIBAN
Ay, that I will and from now on be wiser
And seek God's grace. An ass—six times an ass
Was I—to take this drunkard for a god
And worship this dumb clown!

PROSPERO
                    Enough. Away!

ALONSO
[to Stephano and Trinculo] And go put all these things back
  where you found them. 300

SEBASTIAN
Or stole them from, most likely.

  [Exit CALIBAN, STEPHANO, and TRINCULO
        carrying apparel they stole]

PROSPERO
Your Highness I invite your entourage
And you to my poor lodgings, where you all
May rest tonight, though part of it I'll spend
Relating what no doubt will make the time 305
Pass quickly by—the story of my life,
And the precise events that have occurred
Since I came to this isle. When morning comes,

I'll take you to your ship and on to Naples,
Where I look forward to the solemn rites   310
That bind this dear, belovèd pair in marriage,
At which point I'll withdraw to Mílan where
Each third thought will be of my grave.

ALONSO
                                        I long
To hear the story of your life, which should
Keep us enthralled.

PROSPERO
                        I'll give a full account   315
And promise you calm seas, obliging winds,
And passage that's so expeditious that
You'll catch your fleet. [aside to Ariel] My Ariel, bird,
That is your task. You're free then to rejoin
The elements. Fare well!—[to the others] Please come inside. 320

[Exit]

EPILOGUE

Spoken by PROSPERO

My magic power has reached its end.
On natural strengths I will depend,
Which are quite weak. Now it's true,
I'm either here confined by you
Or sent to Naples. Let me not,   5
Now that my dukedom I have got
And pardoned its usurper, dwell
On this bare island in your spell.
Release me from this narrow band
With help I get from your warm hand.   10
Have your kind breath fill my sails,
It must, or else my project fails,

Which was to please. Now I can't
Summon spirits or enchant,
And my ending is despair   15
Unless I'm rescued by this prayer
That somehow breaches mercy's vault
And I'm forgiven for each fault.
As you absolved of sin would be,
Your generous offering sets me free.   20

THE END

Miranda

Endnotes

About the Play

[1]It is impossible to determine with certainty that Shakespeare knew of the *Sea Venture* story, but most scholars accept it as highly likely. William Strachey, one of the survivors of the shipwreck and a literary figure probably known to Shakespeare, sent a letter back to London that gave an account of the events. The letter was not published until 1625 for political reasons, but it was passed around London and certainly the talk of the town. Ariel's description of the shipwreck has some interesting similarities to Strachey's account of the storm.

You can find the text of Strachey's letter online at the Folger Shakespeare Library or Virtual Jamestown.

[2] In Shakespeare's day, the word *brave* could certainly mean "courageous." But the word could also describe fine dress in the sense of "handsome" or "showy." The *Oxford English Dictionary* cites Shakespeare's *As You Like It* (1600) as the first known use of the term to offer a general description of people in that sense. This meaning for *brave* fell out of use by the end of the 17th century but had a brief revival in the 19th century, perhaps picked up from people reading Shakespeare.

And of course, the title of Aldous Huxley's 1930 novel *Brave New World* quotes Miranda and uses the phrase ironically though not necessarily in the sense that Shakespeare intended. Miranda's statement is taken by many as ironical since the men she observes include several undersirable types. But that view ignores the fact that she is looking at the nobles in their magically preserved finery. She used the same word to describe Ferdinand in Act One. The scruffier characters are not onstage. Miranda certainly does not think Caliban is splendid.

Those who see a more cynical message behind the play may want to argue that the word *brave* had become faddish and overused with Shakespeare poking fun at it as he did with the word *element* in *Twelfth Night*.

Act One

[1]A notoriously difficult passage as Prospero's warning suggests. The issue is whether privacy obscured Prospero's achievements or whether seclusion was merely a drawback. Here is a translation if the second sense is preferred.

> Gaining far more—apart from my seclusion—
> Than popularly thought....

[2] Original: "which raised in me/ An undergoing stomach, to bear up/ Against what should ensue." These lines invite lots of interpretations. I picked up on the metaphor of a woman in labor.

[3] Prospero could be talking about Caliban. In that case, he could say, "That dullard. Who else?"

[4] The original lines where Prospero gives Ariel instructions are laid out as verse but have meter and line length deviations.

> Go make thyself like a nymph o' th' sea; be subject
> To no sight but thine and mine, invisible
> To every eyeball else. Go take this shape,
> And hither come in 't. Go, hence with diligence!

The lines also suggests that the audience will not be able to see Ariel, which is doubtful the case. I took the liberty of adding a stage direction where Prospero hands Ariel a disguise in order to establish for the audience when Ariel is invisible.

[5] Scholars strugggle with with the meaning of Ferdinand's "A single thing, as I am now...."

[6] This person would be Duke Antonio's son and Prospero's nephew. The character never appears in the play and is not mentioned again. The simplest explanation is that Shakespeare decided to omit the character later without correcting this line.

[7] The original: "Make not too rash a trial of him, for/ He's gentle, and not fearful." "Not fearful" is taken by some to mean he is noble and will stand his ground. Some, including Frank Kermode, think Miranda is saying that Ferdinand is gentle and not a threat. The translation then would be, "He's gentle and no threat."

Act Two
[1] Antonio and Sebastian maintain a litany of strained, sarcastic jokes throughout the scene. How much of their banter the others hear has generally been a matter for actors to decide. Certainly Gonzalo hears much of it since he comments on it.

[2] In Shakespeare's time, there was a debate over whether the legendary Greek queen Dido was chaste after the death of her husband or whether she had an illicit affair with Aeneas as described in Virgil's *Aenid*. The narrative Gonzalo seems to favor has Dido committing suicide rather

than being forced into marriage. But his point is that Claribel, like Dido, is a fine queen. The cynical Antonio seems to accept Virgil's more famous account and uses it as fodder for more bad jokes and perhaps a dig at Alonso's daughter who accepted a marriage to someone she did not care for. It is not clear whether Dido and Aeneas lived in the same era. Historical evidence places Dido, if she existed at all, in Carthage around 814 BC. Aeneas had lost his wife during the sacking of Troy. Troy was sacked centuries before Carthage was founded.

[3] In the original, Gonzalo says "I mean, in a sort." He means "in a way" or "more or less." Antonio gives the uninterpretible answer "That sort was well fished for" which may refer to drawing lots.

[4] The original passage is uninterpretable ("Ambition cannot pierce a wink beyond/ But doubt discovery there"). One view is that Antonio's excitement caused him to garble his meaning, prompting Antonio to slow down and explain more carefully what he is suggesting. I added a line by Sebastian to make it clear Antonio's circumlocution has confused Sebastian.

[5] The original word *crab* could refer to sour apples or crabs.

[6] The word *scamels* is unknown and the subject of three hundred years of speculation. It may be a crustacean, a bird that preys upon crustaceans, or some kind of fish. I settled on mussels.

Act Three
[1] The original reads, "There be some sports are painful, and their labor/Delight in them set(s) off." Some see Ferdinand offering a more complicated sentiment than I opted for. One view is that pain provides a background against which the color of pleasure is set off. It is not clear what *set off* means and whether the subject of *set* is *labor* or *delight*.

[2] Shakespeare's "Most busiest when I do it" (or perhaps "Most busy least, when I do it") has no agreed-upon interpretation. Are thoughts of Miranda distracting him from his work or motivating him? I see Ferdinand as apologizing for letting thoughts of Miranda keep him from his work but also recognizing that she gives him the motivation to carry on.

[3] Original: "The folly of this island." The word *folly* could refer to fools, but Frank Kermode and others see it as meaning "freaks". Trinculo could be responding to the word *monster* or looking ahead to his next comment about their stupidity. I kept both meanings.

[4] It is possible that Stephano is asking the malodorous Caliban to move back some. Most editors have the instruction addressed to Trinculo.

[5] In the Folio, these stage directions and the next two stage directions appear here as one stage direction

Act Four

[1] In Shakespeare's day, one hypothesis linked passion to activities of the liver.

[2] The original ("Thy banks with pionèd and twillèd brims") gets nearly six pages of discussion in fine print in the *New Variorium* edition. The *Oxford English Dictionary* cites this as the first use of *pioned* and *twilled* and says that the meanings are uncertain. The sentence perhaps describes some effort at preventing erosion since *brims* was generally used to refer to the edges of lakes or streams.

[3] Editors since Rowe in 1709 have argued over whether the correct word is *wise* or *wife*. Recent study of the typography of the Folio favors *wise*. I arranged a line where those preferring *wife* can substitute it without disturbing the syntax.

[4] It is not clear whether this line is directed to Ferdinand or Miranda. The original "sweet" would perhaps eliminate Ferdinand for modern audiences. "Dear one" leaves it more ambiguous (and corrects the meter).

[5] In the Folio, this stage direction appeared with the previous stage direction.

Act Five

[1] Scholars disagree over whether the line should read "these [Prospero's] words...." instead of the Folio's "their words...." Here is a translation for those favoring "these words." In this emendation, Prospero is reassuring Alonso that he is not a phantom. The preceding punctuation changes to a semi-colon.

> ; these words are made
> By normal breathing.

[2] The original in the Folio reads: "Yes, for a score of kingdoms you should wrangle/ And I would call it fair play." One view argues that

the word *and* should read *an*, meaning "if." Miranda would then be saying that Ferdinand would take twenty kingdoms from her if she did not stop him from cheating. Here is that idea in verse.

> And you would trick me out of twenty kingdoms
> If I thought this fair play.

[3] Is Sebastian being sarcastic or is he truly impressed?

[4] The original line reads "And deal in her command without her power." It's not clear whether the witch had more or less power than the moon.

How Iambic Pentameter Works*

What is iambic pentameter? How does it work? This article explains the basic construction of iambic pentameter as found in the most famous of Shakespeare's plays.[1]

With the exception of the *Merry Wives of Windsor*, which is 90% prose, Shakespeare's plays employ generous servings of a verse line known as *iambic pentameter*. Some of his early plays are almost entirely in this form, and all but four plays are at least 50% verse. So it is useful to understand something of iambic pentameter in order to develop an ear for its complex rhythms and to appreciate its dramatic uses.

What is Iambic Pentameter?

The term iambic pentameter has three parts which together give a rough description of this verse form. The term *meter* refers to a pattern of rhythm. If you pronounce most two-syllable words in a natural way, you will sense a rhythm, with one syllable receiving more energy than the other. Say the words in (1) and note the different rhythms:

(1)   táble (stressed/unstressed)
       prefér (unstressed/stressed)

An accent mark over a vowel indicates that the syllable containing that vowel is pronounced with more energy than the syllable without the accent mark. We call this increased energy *stress*,[2] and an accented syllable is called a *stressed syllable*. Syllables with less energy are called *unstressed*.

Iambic refers to a pattern of meter where an unstressed syllable precedes a stressed syllable. The words in (2) have an iambic rhythm and each forms a metrical unit known as an *iamb*:

(2)   affórd, forbíd, inféct, adópt

Two-word sequences can also have an iambic rhythm.

* Exercises accompany the online version of this article (available at http://www.fullmeasurepress.com/Iambic_Pentameter.html)

(3)   a bít, the mán, to gó, is mád, of míne

The term **penta** (five) tells us how many instances of this iambic rhythm make up a line. Each instance is traditionally called a **foot**, so an iambic pentameter line has five iambic feet, or **iambs**. In these ten-syllable lines of five iambs (4), observe how the even-numbered syllables get more stress than the odd numbered syllables.

(4)   Thy gláss/ will shów/ thee hów/ thy béau/ties wéar/
        1   2   3   4   5 6   7 8   9   10
                                        (Sonnet 77, line 1)
        And cáll/ upón/ my sóul/ withín/ the hóuse/
        1   2   3 4   5 6   7 8   9 10
                                        (Twelfth Night, 1.5.251)
        Beshréw/ that héart/ that mákes/ my héart/ to gróan/
        1 2   3   4   5   6   7   8   9 10
                                        (Sonnet 133, line 1)

We sense that the 2nd, 4th, 6th, 8th, and 10th syllables (marked with ´) receive more emphasis than the 1st, 3rd, 5th, 7th, and 9th syllables. In (5), the line has ten syllables, but notice that it is not iambic pentameter. If we use the jargon of verse analysis, we say the line does not **scan**.

(5)   Récog/níze the/ rhýthm's/ nót i/ámbic/
        1 2   3   4   5 6   7 8 9 10

Here the 1st, 3rd, 5th, 7th, and 9th syllables receive the emphasis. If we placed this line after any of the lines in (4), we would not sense a meter developing and would interpret the passage as prose.

(6)   Thy gláss/ will shów/ thee hów/ thy béau/ties wéar/
        Récog/níze the/ rhýthm's/ nót i/ámbic/

One appealing feature of iambic pentameter is that it sounds like verse yet seems natural. The perfectly iambic lines in (7) were randomly selected from different plays. Read them in sequence and notice how they sound rhythmical without seeming "sing-songy" or bouncy.

(7) Expóse/ thysélf/ to féel/ what wrétch/es féel/
                                          (King Lear, 3.4.39)
     In wóm/en's wáx/en héarts/ to sét/ their fórms/
                                          (Twelfth Night, 2.2.30)
     To bréathe/ such vóws/ as lóv/ers úse/ to swéar/
                                          (Romeo and Juliet, 2. Prologue. 10)

The three lines, though not sing-songy, do sound rhythmically monotonous. Imagine a play with 2,500 such lines pounding away one after the other. The effect would surely be deadening, and dramatists would be severely limited in the kinds of sentences they could write and the vocabulary they could use. So they relax the rules a bit.[3] Most of these deviations fall into two categories: adding extra syllables and altering the iambic meter.

Adding Extra Syllables

There are three common ways to increase the number of syllables beyond ten.

Feminine Endings
     If every line had to end with an iamb, many, if not most, two syllable words—*mother, palace, person, hungry*—could never end a line. So iambic lines allow an extra unstressed eleventh syllable (even a twelfth) at the end of line. This eleventh syllable is called a ***feminine ending***, and about 10% of the lines in Shakespeare's early plays and about 30% in his later plays have such endings. The lines from (4) have been modified to show how the feminine ending sounds.

(8) Thy gláss/ will shów/ thee hów/ thy béau/ties wéath*er*/.
     1   2   3   4   5   6   7   8   9   10 Ø
     And cáll/ upón/ my sóul/ withín/ the pál*ace*/
     Beshréw/ that héart/ that mákes/ my héart/ to súf*fer*/

The words *weather, palace,* and *suffer* provide the 10th and 11th syllables in these lines, but because the 11th is unstressed, the lines still sound iambic to the trained ear. If feminine endings are allowed, then almost any word can be worked into the end of an iambic pentameter line. In fact, we can easily make the un-

metrical line (5) acceptable if we add a syllable at the beginning
of the line to push the stressed syllables into the even-numbered
positions. Since the 11th syllable is unstressed, it counts as a
feminine ending.

(9) *And* réc/ogníze/ the rhýth/m's nów/ iámbic/
  1   2   3   4   5   6   7   8 9 10 Ø

Syllable Deletions
  Lines can also have extra syllables if a syllable can be
dropped without the word becoming unintelligible or sounding
unnatural. Note how many three-syllable words can become
two-syllable words in rapid or slightly slurred speech.

(10) interest (intrist)   Goneril (gonril)
      monument (mon^{y}ment)   Romeo (romyo)
      traveler (travler)   Juliet (Julyet)
      Viola (vyola)   valiant (valyent)

The trick in "scanning" Shakespeare is to anticipate whether
he intends such words to be two or three syllables. As you read
Shakespeare, be prepared for slurrings (traditionally called
elision or **syncope**) that may appear odd, incomprehensible, or
archaic to modern speakers such as *to't* (to it), *e'en* (even), *show'th*
(showeth), *upon't* (upon it), and *lov'st* (lovest).[4]

Epic Caesura
  Lines can have an extra unstressed syllable right before
a major punctuation break, a variation called **epic caesura**
("says you're a..."). Note in (11) that the second syllable of the
word *kingdom* is unstressed and precedes a major punctuation
break. This extra eleventh syllable is not added to the syllable
count, creating a mid-line feminine ending of sorts.

(11)   Know that we have divided
      In three/ our king/~~dom~~; and 'tis/ our fast/ intent/
       1   2   3   4   Ø   5   6   7   8   9 10
                                  (King Lear, 1.1.39-40)

  If we allow a feminine ending, slurring, and epic caesura
in a single line, we can produce a fairly complex line that stays

within the rules of iambic pentameter. How would you scan this thirteen-syllable line (12) from *Twelfth Night*? Is it iambic pentameter?

(12) Even in a minute. So full of shapes is fancy
(Twelfth Night, 1.1.14)

Some scholars question the meter of this line, but here's a try at scanning it. *Even* is slurred to *E'en*. The second, unstressed syllable of *minute* is not counted because it precedes a major punctuation break (epic caesura), and the second, unstressed syllable of *fancy* is a feminine ending.

(13) E'en in/ a min/~~ute~~. So full/ of shapes/ is fancy/
   1 2 3 4   Ø   5 6 7   8   9 10 Ø

Shakespeare is pushing the limits here, especially for contemporary speakers who have trouble slurring *even* to *e'en*, but the line technically qualifies as iambic pentameter.

Altering the Meter

Besides an iambic rhythm, a two-syllable foot can have three other rhythms (see the table on page 142). These rhythms can be worked into an iambic pentameter line in various ways.

Spondees

   A spondaic foot—one where both syllables are likely to be stressed—can occur anywhere. Spondees work at the beginning of a line as these revisions of the lines from (4) show.

(14) ***Bíll's gláss*/** will shów/ thee hów/ thy béau/ties wéar/
    ***Cáll nów*/** upón/ my sóul/ withín/ the hóuse/
    ***Cúrse nót*/** that héart/ that mákes/ my héart/ to gróan/

In (15), spondees (in boldface) are worked into the middle and end of lines.

(15) Thy gláss/ will shów/ **Bíll hów/** thy béau/ties wéar/
    Upón/ my sóul/ withín/ the hóuse,/ ***cáll nów*/**
    Beshréw/ that héart/ that mákes/ ***Bób's héart*/** to
    gróan/

Spondees have an interesting effect: they slow down the line. Speakers need time to give stressed syllables extra energy, so lines filled with spondees have a deliberate, pounding rhythm. A line from *King Lear* demonstrates this clearly.

(16) Nó, nó,/ nó, nó!/ Cóme, lét's/ awáy/ to príson/
(*King Lear, 5.3.9*)

Type of Foot	Rhythm	Single Words	Word Sequences
Trochee	stressed/ unstressed	néver, óffer báttle, únder	whát a, wánt to dróp it
Spondee	stressed/ stressed	cúpcáke súitcáse úpkéep	bád lúck tálks bíg
Pyrrhic Foot	unstressed/ unstressed	suit<u>able</u> hap<u>pily</u> list<u>ening</u>	of a, to it, of the

Trochees

If every iambic pentameter line had to begin with an iamb, then most English words could not start a line. Yet a quick look at Shakespeare's sonnets reveals a different reality. We find these poems start with stressed one-syllable words (*look, when, not, but, let, lord, how, why, full, take, sin, thus, love*), and trochaic two-syllable words (*béing, wéary, músic, Cúpid*)—all words or phrases that start off the line with a stressed syllable.

Iambic pentameter solves this problem by allowing a trochaic rhythm to start a line. These modified versions of (4) are all acceptable iambic pentameter lines.

(17) *Mírrors*/ will shów/ thee hów/ thy béau/ties wéar/
Cálling/ upón/ my sóul/ withín/ the hóuse/
Cúrsing/ that héart/ that mákes/ my héart/ to gróan/

Trochees can also occur in the middle of a line if they follow a strongly stressed syllable or a major punctuation break. In

(18), *haply* has a trochaic rhythm, but it is allowed because it follows a major punctuation break. It also follows the heavily stressed word *all.*

(18)   They lóve/ you áll?/ ***Háply**/*, when I/ shall wéd/
(King Lear, 1.1.110)

Phrases that appear to be trochaic are permitted if they fall within a sequence of one-syllable words. In the 3rd foot of (19), we would normally expect the word *love* to get more emphasis than *which*, yielding the trochaic rhythm *lóve, which.*

(19)   A bróth/er's déad/ ***lóve, which**/* she would/ kéep frésh/
(Twelfth Night, 1.1.30)

This reading sounds like prose. But notice that the word *which* is surrounded by one-syllable words. In this environment, rarely-stressed words such as *the, which, of, is,* and *been* can be stressed to preserve an iambic rhythm, without sounding unnatural, as in (21).

(20)   A bróth/er's déad/ love, whích/ she wóuld/ keep frésh/

Actors may choose not to give the line an iambic rhythm, but the fact that they can qualifies the line as iambic pentameter. (See "Listening for Phrasal Stress" on page 148).

Pyrrhic Feet
Normally, pyrrhic feet do not cause a problem. A foot with two unstressed syllables glides right by without upsetting the meter. The lines in (21) show typical uses of pyrrhic feet (in bold italics).

(21)   For she/ did speak/ in starts/ distract***/edly**/*
She loves/ me sure./ The cun***/ning of**/* her passion/
Invites/ in me/ this chur/lish mes***/senger**. */
(Twelfth Night, 2.2.20-22)

Unmetrical Lines

If trochaic, spondaic, and pyrrhic feet can come anywhere in a line, then wouldn't just about any ten-syllable line be iambic pentameter? Actually, the meter is more restricted than it appears because of one rule: a word with a trochaic rhythm cannot fill the 2nd, 3rd, 4th, or 5th foot unless a stressed syllable or a major punctuation break precedes that foot. Sounds complicated, but that is the rule violated by the positioning of *dinner* in (22).[5]

(22) Áft**er/ dínner/** he wálked/ acróss/ the stréet/
     1 2   3 4   5 6   7 8   9 10

The *-ter* of *after* and the first syllable of the trochaic word *dínner* cannot be in two separate feet because that leaves the stressed syllable of *dinner* in an odd-numbered position surrounded by two unstressed syllables. Forcing the two-syllable word *dinner* into an iambic rhythm is too unnatural, something on the order of *d'nér*. To fix this line, we need to nudge the first syllable of *dinner* into an even-numbered position. Here are several possibilities.

(23) He áft/er dín/ner wálked/ acróss/ the róad/
        He wálked/ 'cross th' róad/ right áf/ter dín/ner, sír/

The second line requires two elisions—*'cross* and *th' road*. My translations avoid odd-looking elisions like *th' road*, but be ready for them if you delve into the original. Can you figure out these? *Woo't, 'a, s', to't, tak'n, sev'n, within's.* (Answers: *wouldst thou, he, his, to it, taken, seven, within this*).

Regardless of what precedes it, we rarely find a word with a trochaic rhythm filling the last foot. Line (24), like (22), is unmetrical and interpreted as prose, not verse.

(24) He wálked/ acróss/ the róad/ to éat /**dínner/**

Line (24) can be corrected if we force a feminine ending by adding an extra syllable, in this case the word *his*.

(25) He wálked/ acróss/ the róad/to éat/his dínner/
       1 2   3 4   5 6   7 8   9 10 Ø

Verse vs. Prose

To highlight the difference between verse and prose, let's mechanically divide a prose passage from *King Lear* into ten-syllable lines. Even with slurring and long lines, only the lines in ***bold italics*** seem acceptable iambic pentameter, and some of these require uncharacteristic and rather clumsy breaks in the syntax at the end of lines. The other lines all deviate from Shakespeare's usual verse.

(26) **EDMUND**
This is the exc'llent fopp'ry of the world
That, when we are sick in fortune—often
The surfeit of our own behaviour—we
Make guilty of our disasters the sun,
The moon, and the stars; as if we were villains
On necessity; fools by heavenly
Compulsion; knaves, thieves, and treachers by spherical
Pre-dominance; drunkards, liars, and adulterers
By an enforcéd obedience of
Planetary influence; and all that
We are evil in, by a divine thrusting
On: an admirable evasion of whoremaster
Man, to lay his goatish disposition
To the charge of a star! My father compounded
With my mother under the dragon's tail
And my nativity was under Ursa
Major; so that it follows I am rough
And lecherous.—Tut! I should have been that
I am, had the maidenliest star in
The firmament twinkled on my bastardizing.
(King Lear, 1.2.125-140)

All told, only five out of twenty lines can be read as verse, and that is why Edmund's speech is always formatted as prose.

Let's compare Edmund's prose soliloquy to a passage that certainly complicates the iambic pattern yet is always formatted as verse. I have highlighted with ***bold italics*** some of the more difficult lines to scan.

(27) **LEAR**
Peace, Kent!
Come not between the dragon and his wrath.
I loved her most, and thought to set my rest
On her kind nursery.—Hence, and avoid my sight!
So be my grave my peace, as here I give
Her father's heart from her!—Call France—who stirs?
Call Burgundy!—Cornwall and Albany,
With my two daughters' dowers digest this third:
        [*dowers* is slurred to one-syllable]
Let pride, which she calls plainness, marry her.
I do invest you jointly in my power,
Pre-eminence, and all the large effects
That troop with majesty.—Ourself, by monthly course,
        [long line]
With reservation of an hundred knights,
By you to be sustained, shall our abode
Make with you by due turns. Only we still retain [long]
The name, and all th' additions to a king;
The sway, revénue, execution of the rest, [long]
Belovèd sons, be yours; which to confirm,
This coronet part betwixt you....[*coronet* slurred]

KENT
        Royal Lear,
        (King Lear, 1.1.135-155)

This passage is about as wild as Shakespeare's iambic pentameter gets, yet only five of the eighteen lines are difficult to scan. Three are long lines (hexameters), more frequent in Shakespeare's later plays, and the other two deviant lines have rather complicated rhythms, perhaps to signal that Lear is yelling and losing his temper. The last line is an example of a ***shared line*** where one speaker finishes the line by responding to or overlapping the previous speaker.

    This comparison shows that iambic pentameter is not prose and that verse dramatists are quite aware when they are shifting between verse and prose (even if many modern actors obscure the difference). It also shows that iambic pentameter, while it allows for deviation in line length and rhythm, imposes constraints on a line.

Verse Reading Tips

Verse and Prose

To become more aware of when Shakespeare is using verse or prose, pay attention to how editors format the lines. In verse passages, all lines begin with a capital letter and long lines have a hanging indent.

(28)
HORATIO
What art thou that usurp'st this time of night,
Together with that fair and warlike form
In which the majesty of buried Denmark
Did sometimes march? By heav'n, I charge
    thee speak.

MARCELLUS
It is offended.

BARNARDO
        See it stalks away.
                (*Hamlet*, 1.1.54-58)

Marcellus and Bernardo are sharing a line of verse, so Bernardo's line is tabbed over to show that he is finishing the line started by Marcellus. Prose passages, on the other hand, do not have hanging indents and use normal capitalization rules:

(29)
HAMLET
Speak the speech, I pray you, as I pronounced it to you trippingly on the tongue; but if you mouth it, as many of our players do, I had as lief the town-crier spoke my lines. Nor do not saw the air too much with your hand, thus, but use all gently; for in the very torrent, tempest, and, as I may say, whirlwind of your passion, you must acquire and beget a temperance that may give it smoothness....
                (*Hamlet*, 3.2.1-8)

Listening for Phrasal Stress

Shakespeare took the trouble to write most of his dialog in verse, and most of his verse lines hold to the meter. So to get a feel for Shakespeare's language, it helps to do some scanning as you read. But be warned, scanning is more than a simple mechanical process.

Line (30) is an easy line to scan because Shakespeare placed content-heavy words—*jest, scars, never, felt, wound*— in the stressed positions.

(30) He jésts/ at scárs/ that név/er félt/ a wóund./
(*Romeo and Juliet*, 2.2.1)

The less important words that provide the glue that holds the sentence together—*he, at, that, a*—and the second syllable of *never* comfortably fall into the unstressed positions. Does a strategy of placing stress on content-heavy words always work?

English has a feature of pronunciation called **phrasal stress** (or **rhetorical stress** when applied to meter) that complicates scanning. Phrasal stress allows the speaker to give extra stress to the most important word in a phrase or sentence. This extra emphasis by default will appear near the end of a phrase, especially if the words are rather equal in importance. If you say the line in (31) with normal emphasis (assuming you do not speak in a monotone), you will hear the pitch of your voice rise and fall as you say the word *wound*.

(31) He jésts at scárs that néver félt a **wóund**.

Phrasal stress explains why longer words, when spoken in isolation, seem to have one syllable with extra emphasis (see Exercise 1b).

(32)   éstimátion
       óverlóok

In actual sentences, though, this phantom stress may disappear.

(33) To be of worth and worthy éstimátion
                    (*Two Gentleman of Verona*, 2.4)
      Of éstimátion and command in **árms**.
                    (*Henry IV, part I*, 4.4)

In the first line, we sense that the second stress in *estimation* is stronger because the word is likely to receive phrasal stress. In the second line, the two stressed syllables in *estimation* seem about the same if the phrasal stress falls later in the sentence.

Phrasal stress does not have to land at the end of a sentence. Speakers can place it on whatever word they feel is most important. That means phrasal stress does not always fall on a content word. You can see this possibility in the way we respond to statements and questions.

(34)   A: Did you spill it? B:No, **hé** spilled it.
        A: I hear you're now a manager. B: No, I'm **thé** manager.
        A: You're not serious. B: I **ám** serious.

Here the new or unpredictable information is not found in content-heavy words. So if you scan by simply adding emphasis to any content-heavy word, you may be missing the emphasis that Shakespeare intended.

Sometimes Shakespeare takes advantage of the iambic rhythm itself to draw attention to a word we might not normally stress. Take a look at the boldfaced feet in this passage from Act 3 of *Hamlet*. Normally the content words *tempt*, *call*, and *make* would get more stress, but here the meter suggests that Shakespeare wants the actor playing Hamlet to emphasize the word *you*. He does this by placing the word *you* in a position where the meter pulls us to add extra emphasis.

(35) Not this by no means that I bid you do:
Let the/ bloat king/ **tempt yóu**/ again/ to bed,/
Pinch wan/ton on/ your cheek,/ **call yóu**/ his mouse,/
And let him, for a pair of reechy kisses
Or paddling in your neck with his damned fingers,
Make yóu/ to rav/el all/ this mat/ter out/
                    (*Hamlet*, 3.4.203-208)

This analysis is speculative, of course but seems a likely example of Shakespeare's artful use of iambic pentameter.

The speaker's attitude and emotional state can also influence phrasal stress. Actors, of course, will be on the lookout for such clues and play with phrasal stress to supply this kind of information about the character they are playing. Take a look at a line we studied before. The punctuation on the printed page suggests six likely phrasal stresses (boldfaced).

(36) **Nó, nó,**/ **nó, nó.**/ **Cóme,** lét's/ awáy/ to **prís**/on.
(King Lear, 5.3.9)

An actor playing an angry Lear might prefer pounding out these phrasal stresses with a series of spondees. But what if he sees Lear as resigned to his fate and calmly dismissing the preceding question? He then may choose to skip along more quickly and land phrasal stress on the 2nd and 4th *noes.*

(37) Nó, **nó,**/ nó, **nó.**/ **Cóme,** lét's/ awáy/ to **prís**on/

And what is the effect if the actor raises the pitch of his voice on the 1st and 3rd *noes*?

(38) **Nó,** nó,/ **nó,** nó./ **Cóme,** lét's/ awáy/ to **prís**/on

As readers or actors, where we place phrasal stress can affect both the rhythm and meaning of a line. That is why scanning a line of verse is challenging and involves more than a mechanical process.

Keep in mind, though, that phrasal stress and metrical stress usually coincide—good writing generally requires it—and that mechanical approaches for scanning lines are helpful. Shakespeare no doubt counted syllables and tapped out meter in his head. Just remember that two language phenomena are at work. Metrical stress establishes an underlying rhythm by taking advantage of how we normally pronounce words. Phrasal (or rhetorical) stress concerns a decision as to what word is most important or unpredictable in a phrase. Consider both when scanning a line.

Scanning Exercise

Here is the untranslated version of Duke Orsino's famous opening speech in *Twelfth Night*. Scholars have argued that the meter is as fickle and impulsive as the Duke himself, with smooth, flowing phrases interrupted by spondaic rhythms.

Try scanning it. You should find at least one example of all the metrical variations described in this article. I have added several stress marks to show how Shakespeare most likely pronounced the words.

DUKE ORSINO

If music be the food of love, play on.

Give me excéss of it, that, súrfeiting,

The appetite may sicken and so die.

That strain again! It had a dying fall.

O, it came o'er my ear like the sweet sound

That breathes upon a bank of violets,

Stealing and giving odor. Enough; no more.

'Tis not so sweet now as it was before.

O spirit of love, how quick and fresh art thou!

That, notwithstanding thy capacity

Receiveth as the sea, nought enters there,

Of what validity and pitch soé'er,

But falls into abatement and low price,

Even in a minute. So full of shapes is fancy

That it alone is high fantastical.

Notes

[1] Shakespeare's use of iambic pentameter did not remain consistent over his career. In his later plays, such as *Coriolanus*, expect more deviations from the rather tight rules described here. And recognize that Shakespeare was not required to write blank verse and that his plays will mix verse and prose. He was also no perfectionist and did not provide careful editions of his work. Expect as you read a play to

see the work of scholars who have done the editing that Shakespeare failed to do. Faulty meter is often corrected or "emended." The more detailed editions will painstakingly list all these changes and the justifications for them.

[2] We perceive stress as extra energy. The reality is a bit more complicated. Stress can be achieved by an increase in volume, a lengthening of the syllable itself, a pause after a syllable, a rise in pitch, or even a change in the timbre of one's voice. It may be a combination of these.

[3] Think of the term "rule" as meaning constraints on the patterns of rhythm that Shakespeare tended to employ when he wrote blank verse. Or think of these rules more simply as a description of what Shakespeare typically did or typically did not do. Shakespeare, of course, could ignore these rules whenever he wished to, but there is no doubt that Shakespeare placed constraints on what he typically allowed in a verse line. He most certainly counted syllables. Though he experimented with ways of stretching the boundaries of blank verse, he did not write free verse. Some of his prose passages may have a free verse feel. For a technical description of the rule-governed approach that underlies my description of Shakespeapere's verse, see the Wikipedia article on "Generative Metrics."

[4] Occasionally Shakespeare will coax an extra syllable out of a word. *Entrance* becomes something more like *ent-er-ance*. *Fire* seems more like *fi-yer* and *cruel* more like *cru-el*.

[5] I gleaned this rule from a 1975 paper by linguist Paul Kiparsky. He was improving upon the work in generative metrics by Morris Halle, Samuel Jay Keyser, Joseph Beaver, and others. Although I avoid the technical jargon of Halle and Keyser's approach and use the terminology of traditional metrics, I am much influenced by their work. If you are interested in this very technical approach, see the Wikipedia article on iambic pentameter or the article on generative metrics. Kiparsky's article is available on *JSTOR*. And here's a website on iambic pentameter (http://shakespeare.wikia.com/wiki/Iambic_pentameter) that acknowledges Halle and Keyser's contribution and explains their concept of the *stress maxima*. Halle and Keyser developed a clever tool for tabulating the complexity of a metrical line.

[6] Some, particularly George T. Wright in his *Shakespeare's Metrical Art*, seem to resist and dismiss precise rules for spotting unmetrical lines. Wright seems to be arguing that a line such as

(39) Hé and/ Lépid/us are/ at Caes/ar's house.

(Julius Caesar, 3.2.264)

with its double trochee in the first two feet is not unmetrical, just very rare. But such rhythms are only rare when one is writing iambic pentamenter, so it seems safe to say that Shakespeare either wrote an unmetrical line or was writing prose.

Wright even lists the opening line of the John Keats sonnet (40) as metrical. But I understand the line to be a metrical joke, where Keats purposely disrupts the rhythm in the 3rd and 4th feet to pun on "lapses of time."

(40) How man/y bards/ gíld the/ lápses/ of time!
    A few of them have ever been the food
    Of my delighted fancy,—I could brood
Over their beauties, earthly, or sublime:
And often, when I sit me down to rhyme,
    These will in throngs before my mind intrude:
    But no confusion, no disturbance rude
Do they occasion; 'tis a pleasing chime.
So the unnumbered sounds that evening store;
    The songs of birds—the whispering of the leaves—
    The voice of waters—the great bell that heaves
With solemn sound,—and thousand others more,
    That distance of recognizance bereaves,
Makes pleasing music, and not wild uproar.

Wright seems a bit stubborn here. A lapse in time is a lapse in time.

Keep in mind that poets are not obligated to mimic the way Shakespeare employed iambic pentameter. Poets do not have to advertise what meter they are using and may loosen or tighten the reins a bit or mix types. In "Elegy Written in a Country Churchyard" (41), Thomas Gray (1716-1771) seems to prefer a straightforward, undisguised iambic pentameter, similar to the verse in Shakespeare's early plays, with most lines ending where we would naturally pause (**_end-stopped_** to use the jargon of metrical analysis):

(41) The curfew tolls the knell of parting day,
The lowing herd wind slowly o'er the lea,
The plowman homeward plods his weary way
And leaves the world to darkness and to me....

Others may merely flirt with iambic pentameter or make it quite complex. "Holy Sonnet 14" by John Donne (1572-1631) certainly pushes the limits. Besides the rough and tumble meter, he breaks the 1st and 3rd lines mid-phrase ("for you/ As yet"; "and bend/ Your force"). This device, called ***enjambment***, has the effect of disguising the iambic pentameter a bit. Shakespeare used enjambment more and more frequently as his career proceeded.

> (42) Batter my heart, three-personed God; for You
> As yet but knock, breathe, shine, and seek to mend;
> That I may rise, and stand, o'erthrow me, and bend
> Your force, to break, blow, burn, and make me new.
> I, like an usurped town, to another due,
> Labor to admit You, but oh! to no end.
> Reason, Your viceroy in me, me should defend,
> But is captived, and proves weak or untrue.
> Yet dearly I love You, and would be loved fain,
> But am betrothed unto Your enemy;
> Divorce me, untie, or break that knot again,
> Take me to You, imprison me, for I,
> Except You enthrall me, never shall be free,
> Nor ever chaste, except You ravish me.

Sources

Editions of the Play

The Annotated Shakespeare. 2006. Burton Raffel, ed. New Haven and London: Yale University Press.

The Arden Shakespeare. 1999, 2011. Virginia Mason Vaughan and Alden T. Vaughan, ed. London: Bloomsbury Publishing Plc.

The Folger Shakespeare Library. 1993. Barbara A. Mowat and Paul Werstine, eds. New York: Simon and Schuster.

The Kittredge Shakespeare. 1939. George L. Kittredge. Boston, New York, etc.: Ginn.

The New Cambridge Shakespeare. 2002. David Lindley, ed. Cambridge: Cambridge University Press.

A New Variorium Edition of Shakespeare: Hamlet. 1892. Horace Howard Furness, ed. Philadelphia: J.B. Lippincott & Co.

A Norton Critical Edition. 2011. Peter Hulme and William H. Sherman, eds. New York and London: W.W. Norton & Co.

The Norton Shakespeare: Based on the Oxford Edition, 2nd Edition. 2008, 1997. S. Greenblatt, W. Cohen, J. E. Howard, and K. E. Maus, eds. New York and London: W.W. Norton & Co.

Oxford School Shakespeare. 1998, 2001, 2006. Roma Gill, ed. Oxford: Oxford University Press.

The Oxford Shakespeare. 1987, 2008. Stephen Orgel, ed. Oxford: Oxford University Press.

The Riverside Shakespeare. 1997. Boston and New York: Houghton Mifflin Company.

The RSC Shakespeare. 2007. Jonathan Bate and Eric Rasmussen, eds. New York: The Modern Library.

Shakespeare: Major Plays and the Sonnets. 1948. G.B. Harrison, ed. New York: Harcourt, Brace, and World, inc.

Other Sources

Abbott, E. A. *A Shakespearian Grammar.* 2003. Mineola, New York: Dover Publications, Inc.

Crystal, David and Ben Crystal. *Shakespeare's Words: A Glossary and Language Companion.* 2002. London: Penguin Books.

Compact Edition of the Oxford English Dictionary. 1971. Oxford University Press.

Onions, C.T. *A Shakespeare Glossary.* 1986. Revised and enlarged by Robert D. Eagleson.

Schmidt, Alexander. 1971. *Shakespeare Lexicon and Quotation Dictionary, Volumes 1 and 2.* New York: Dover Publications.

ENJOY SHAKESPEARE

Hamlet
Julius Caesar
King Lear
Macbeth
Much Ado About Nothing
Romeo and Juliet
The Tempest
Twelfth Night

Check for new titles at www.FullMeasurePress.com

www.ingramcontent.com/pod-product-compliance
Lightning Source LLC
Chambersburg PA
CBHW060255050426
42448CB00009B/1654